Turbocharge Your GMAT Math Study Guide

Version 10.1

- ☐ *Math Key Glossary*
- ☐ *Formulae Cheat-Sheet*
- ☐ *Topic by Topic Guide*
    - *Number Properties Guide*
    - *Arithmetic & Algebra*
    - *Geometry, Statistics & Probability*
    - *Permutation / Combinatorics*
- ☐ *Word Problem Framework*
- ☐ *Data Sufficiency Strategies*
- ☐ *Practice Problems by Topic*
- ☐ *Bonus Chapter*
    - *MBA Admissions in a Nutshell*

www.manhattanreview.com

Copyright and Terms of Use

10-Digit International Standard Book Number: (ISBN: 0-9824324-0-2)
13-Digit International Standard Book Number: (ISBN: 978-0-9824324-0-2)

Last updated on February 9, 2010.

GMAT/TOEFL/SAT/LSAT/GRE Prep   MBA/College Admissions   Career Training

Special Valued Customer Reward – 10%/15%

Please come to our free info sessions either online or in-person! As a token of our appreciation of your attendance, we will offer you an exciting new Valued Customer Reward – 10% off any of our courses or services or 15% off any combination of our different courses and services!

How does it work?

- Register for any of free our in-person or online info sessions online or by calling our offices

- Show up and participate in the entire info session

- Your presenter will share with you the coupon codes

- Visit our website at www.ManhattanReview.com! (click on the country website if you are located outside of the US)

- Choose your desired in-person/online course or services such as private tutoring or admissions advisory packages

- If you pay by cash, check or wire transfer, just email us with the coupon code

- If you pay by credit card, just enter the coupon code on the payment page

Additional Notes

- The 10% coupon code is valid for each separate registration for one of our courses or services.

- The 15% coupon code is valid for a combined registration of two or more of any of our courses (different course format) and services (different service type).

- One student per coupon; Cannot be combined with any other coupon or discount certificate for the same course/service

- Valid for a limited time per our announcement at the event

- Test prep course and service availability varies by location

- Other terms and conditions may apply.

Achieve YOUR HIGHER SCORE and get into TOP SCHOOLS!
Visit Manhattan Review NOW to invest in your future!

Turbocharge Your TOEFL Series

- □ **Integrated Study Guide (ISBN: 0-9788435-9-2)**

Turbocharge Your GMAT Series

- √ **Math Study Guide (ISBN: 0-9824324-0-2)**
- □ **Math Study Companion (ISBN: 0-9824324-1-0)**
- □ **Verbal Study Guide (ISBN: 0-9824324-2-9)**
- □ **Verbal Study Companion (ISBN: 0-9824324-3-7**

Manhattan Review Courses & Services

GMAT Courses & Services

- Crash Courses (Major International Cities; 16 Hours one 2-day Weekend;)
- Intensive Courses (Selected Locations; 28 Hours 1-week + 100 Hours Online Library)
- Long Courses (Selected Locations; 28 Hours 8 or 6 Sessions + 100 Hours Online Library)
- Online Courses – Anywhere (Global Access; 28 Hours 9-week + 100 Hours Online Library)
- Private Tutoring (Selected Locations; Advanced Pack - 10 Hours Tutoring + 100 Hours Online Library)
- Online Recording Library – Anywhere (Global Access)

MBA & College Admissions Services (Grad School / Law School Admissions Also Available)

- Elite School Dedicated Pack (Global)
- Application Strategy Advisory Service (Global)
- Resume & Essay Review (Global)
- Mock Interview & Case Interview (Selected Locations)

TOEFL/SAT Courses & Services (GRE/LSAT Tutoring Available)

- Crash Courses (Major International Cities; 16 Hours one 2-day Weekend)
- Long Courses (Selected Locations; 40 Hours 8 Sessions + 20 Hours Online Library)
- Intensive Courses (Selected Locations; 40 Hours 1-week + 20 Hours Online Library)
- Online Courses – Anywhere (Global Access, 24-36 Hours 6-12 week + 20 Hours Online Library)
- Private Tutoring (Selected Locations; Advanced Pack - 10 Hours Tutoring + 20 Hours Online Library)

MBA Training & Management Certificates

Communication Courses

- Presentational Skills
- Business English
- Cultural Sensitivity & Etiquette
- Max Verbal IQ

Foundational Courses

- Excel for Productivity
- Negotiation & Decision Making
- Corporate Finance
- Micro & Macro Economics
- Marketing
- Managerial Accounting
- Capital Markets & Trading Essentials
- Financial Statement Analysis
- Effective Sales
- Computer/MS Office Skills

Management Courses

- Innovation Management
- Talent Management
- Change Management
- Project Management
- Exceptional Customer Service
- Managing International Project Team
- Entrepreneurship
- Effective Leadership
- Corporate Law
- Investment Banking Essentials

Special Seminars

- Basic & Business Chinese
- Interview Skills
- Supply Chain Management
- Operations Management
- Decision Models

Free Seminars, Events & Online Resources

- How to Get Into A Top College
- How to Get Into A Top MBA Program
- TOEFL Overview & Strategies
- GMAT Overview & Strategies
- SAT Overview & Strategies
- MBA Gate School Fairs

Manhattan Review Advantages

- **Time Efficiency and Cost Effectiveness**
  - The most limiting factor in test preparation for most people is time.
  - It takes significantly more teaching experience and techniques to prepare a student in less time.
  - Our preparation is tailored for busy professionals. We will teach you what you need to know in the least amount of time.

- **High-quality and dedicated instructors who are committed to helping every student reach her/his goals**

- **Manhattan Review's team members have combined wisdom of**
  - Academic achievements
  - MBA teaching experiences at prestigious business schools in the US and UK
  - Career success

- **Our curriculum & proprietary Turbocharge Your GMAT course materials**
  - About 600 pages of well-illustrated and professionally presented strategies and exclusive problems for both the Verbal Section and Quantitative Sections
  - 200+ pages of detailed solutions
  - 300 pages of internally developed Quantitative and Verbal vocabulary list with detailed definitions, related words and sentence examples
  - Challenging Online CATs (Included in any course payments; Available for separate purchases)
  - The Official Guide For GMAT Review, Official Guide for GMAT Quantitative Review and Official Guide for GMAT Verbal Review (Available at about 25% discount off regular retial price)

- **Combine with Private Tutoring for a more tailored study package**

- **Special Offer for Our Online Recording Library (Visit Online Library on our website!)**

- **High-quality Career, MBA & College Advisory Full Service**

- **Our Pursuit of Excellence in All Areas of Our Service**

Visit us often at www.ManhattanReview.com!
(Select International Locations for your local content!)

About the Company

Manhattan Review is a multi-national educational services firm, founded by Dr. Joern Meissner in 1999. We are the **only** test prep and management training firm:

- focuses on helping you achieve the **highest test scores (GMAT, TOEFL, SAT/ACT, LSAT, GRE)** with the **least** amount of time and financial **investments**
- supports you **before, during and after MBA** programs with a full range of GMAT courses, MBA Admissions advisory services and Management Training courses
- whose founder is a professor and has extensive experience teaching MBAs at **Ivy League business schools**
- whose instructors include many **top school Ph.D. graduates** with substantial college-level teaching experience and accomplished **MBA graduates with 99th percentile** test scores

Dr. Joern Meissner, the founder of Manhattan Review, has over fifteen years of teaching experience in undergraduate and graduate programs at prestigious business schools in the USA, UK and Germany. He created the original lectures, which have been expanded and modified by the Manhattan Review Team to reflect the evolving nature of the GMAT. Dr. Meissner received his Ph.D. in Management Science from Graduate School of Business at Columbia University (Columbia Business School) in New York City and is a recognized authority in the area of Supply Chain Management (SCM), Dynamic Pricing and Revenue Management. He frequently advises companies ranging from Fortune 500 to emerging start-ups on various issues related to his research expertise. His academic homepage is www.meiss.com.

Tracy C. Yun serves as CEO of Manhattan Review and is also an advisory partner in a boutique investment banking firm. She has over ten years of experience in Mergers & Acquisitions, Restructuring, Bankruptcy and Litigation Consulting. Her industry experience includes Telecom, Technology, General Industrial, Healthcare, Consumer Growth, among others. Ms. Yun scored in the 99th percentile on the GMAT and subsequently received her MBA in Finance and Accounting from Graduate School of Business at Columbia University (Columbia Business School). She oversees Manhattan Review's current management and teaching staff.

International Phone Numbers

US & Canada	(888) 662-6738	UK	20 3318 3131
Germany	(089) 54998 6551	Switzerland	(043) 500 0757
Netherlands	(02) 070 840 87	Belgium	(02) 403 49 84
France	(01)70 61 75 12	Ireland	(01) 44 03 960
Spain	091 789 7270	Sweden	40 62 71 651
Italy	(02) 3601 1780	Hungary	(07) 7999354
Poland	22 48 91 658	Singapore	3106 2069
Japan	3 45 50 12 54	India	40 4241 7788
Hong Kong	36 78 67 53	Rest of World	+1 212 997 1660

Contents

1 GMAT and Its Relevance **1**

1.1 Overview of GMAT 1

1.2 GMAT Scores and Sections 2

1.3 GMAT Preparation and Test-taking Logistics 2

1.4 Quantitative Section 3

1.5 Key Preparation and Test-taking Strategies 4

2 Key Glossary **8**

2.1 Arithmetic 9

2.2 Algebra 12

2.3 Geometry 14

2.4 Coordinate Geometry 17

2.5 Word Problems 18

2.6 Statistics 19

2.7 Combinatorics & Probability 20

3 Formulae Cheatsheet **22**

3.1 Arithmetic 22

3.2 Algebra 23

3.3 Geometry 23

3.4 Word Problems 25

3.5 Statistics 26

3.6 Combinatorics 26

3.7 Probability 26

4 Quick Reference 27
4.1 Multiplication Table . . . 27
4.2 Decimals and Fractions . . . 27
4.3 Squares and Square Roots . . . 28
4.4 Powers of 2 & 3 . . . 28
4.5 Cubes and Cube Roots . . . 28
4.6 Powers of 10 . . . 29
4.7 Factorials . . . 29
4.8 Conversions and Measurements . . . 30
4.8.1 Length . . . 30
4.8.2 Area . . . 30
4.8.3 Volume . . . 30
4.8.4 Mass and Weight . . . 30
4.8.5 Temperature . . . 30
4.8.6 Approximations . . . 31

5 Arithmetic 32
5.1 Basic Concepts in Arithmetic . . . 32
5.1.1 Types of Numbers . . . 32
5.1.2 Fundamental Operations . . . 33
5.2 Number Properties . . . 34
5.2.1 Determining Factors . . . 37
5.2.2 Divisibility of Numbers . . . 37
5.2.3 Chunking . . . 40
5.2.4 Long Division . . . 40
5.2.5 The SMART Algorithm . . . 41
5.2.6 Factorization Algorithm . . . 45
5.3 Fractions . . . 47
5.3.1 Types of Fractions . . . 47
5.3.2 Adding and Subtracting Fractions . . . 48
5.3.3 Equivalent Fractions . . . 48

5.3.4 Multiplying and Dividing Fractions 49
5.3.5 Comparing Fractions 50
5.4 Decimals 51
5.4.1 Introduction to Decimals 51
5.4.2 Scientific Notation 51
5.4.3 Changing Decimals to Fractions 51
5.4.3.1 Terminating Decimals 51
5.4.3.2 Infinite Repeating Decimals 52
5.4.4 Operations with Decimals 53
5.4.4.1 Addition 53
5.4.4.2 Subtraction 53
5.4.4.3 Multiplication 53
5.4.4.4 Division 53
5.5 Real Numbers 54
5.5.1 Introduction 54
5.6 Percentages and Interest 55
5.6.1 Percentage of and Percent Change 55
5.6.2 Interest 56

6 Algebra **58**
6.1 Basic Concepts in Algebra 58
6.2 Taking a SHOT at the Questions 59
6.3 Do Not Multiply Out Intermediate Calculations 60
6.4 Avoid Working with Large Numbers 60
6.5 Algebra SHOTS 62
6.5.1 Manipulation of Equations 62
6.5.2 Manipulation of Inequalities 63
6.6 Systems of Linear Equations 64
6.7 Quadratic Equations 66
6.8 Exponents & Roots 68
6.8.1 Exponents 68
6.8.2 Roots 69
6.8.3 Formulae Review 70

7 Geometry **72**

7.1 Basic Concepts in Geometry 72

7.2 Properties of Angles 73

7.3 Triangles 74

7.3.1 Right Triangle Relationships 75

7.3.2 The Pythagorean Theorem 76

7.3.3 Scalene Triangles 77

7.3.4 Formulae Review 77

7.4 The Equation of a Line 78

7.4.1 Coordinate Geometry 78

7.5 Quadrilaterals 79

7.6 Other Polygons 80

7.6.1 Terminology of Polygons 80

7.7 Circles 81

7.8 Polygons Inscribed In Circles 82

7.9 Three-Dimensional Figures 82

7.10 Properties of Similar Figures 84

7.11 Extending or Adding Lines 84

8 Word Problems **86**

8.1 Translation 86

8.2 Dimensional Analysis 87

8.3 Ratio Problems 88

8.4 Rate Problems 89

8.5 Exponential Growth 90

8.6 Questions with Missing Information 91

8.7 Mixtures 93

9 Statistics **95**

9.1 Sets 95

9.2 Arithmetic Mean 95

9.2.1 Determining Averages 95

9.3 Mode 97

9.4 Median 97

9.5 Range 98

9.6 Standard Deviation 98

10 Combinatorics **100**

10.1 The Basic Idea 100

10.2 Permutations 101

10.3 Combinations 102

10.4 Identical Objects 103

10.5 Circular Arrangements 103

10.6 Advanced Topics 104

11 Probability **106**

11.1 The Basic Idea 106

11.2 Terminology 107

11.3 Dependent and Independent Events 107

11.4 Two Overlapping Events 108

11.5 Three Overlapping Events 109

11.6 Test Taking Hints 110

12 Data Sufficiency **112**

12.1 The Answer Choices 112

12.2 The Three Questions You Must Ask 113

12.3 Read Carefully and Assume Nothing 114

13 MBA Admissions in a Nutshell **117**

13.1 Overview of MBA . . . 117

13.1.1 Why MBA . . . 117

13.1.2 Academic Offerings . . . 118

13.1.3 Pre-MBA Checklist . . . 119

13.2 Program Types . . . 119

13.2.1 Traditional Model . . . 119

13.2.2 Accelerated Programs . . . 120

13.2.3 Part-Time MBA . . . 120

13.2.4 Dual Degree MBA . . . 121

13.2.5 Distance Learning . . . 122

13.3 MBA Programs . . . 122

13.3.1 US MBA Programs . . . 122

13.3.2 International MBA Programs . . . 123

13.3.3 MBA Rankings . . . 124

13.4 Application Strategy . . . 124

13.4.1 Where to Apply . . . 125

13.4.2 When to Apply . . . 126

13.4.3 Program Materials . . . 127

13.4.4 Talking to the Right People . . . 127

13.4.5 MBA Books and Forums . . . 128

13.4.6 Funding Options . . . 128

13.4.7 Women Applying for MBA . . . 129

13.5 MBA Applications . . . 129

13.5.1 Application Form . . . 130

13.5.2 Transcripts and Test Scores . . . 130

13.5.3 Resume . . . 131

13.5.4 Recommendations . . . 132

13.5.5 Essays . . . 133

13.5.6 Interview . . . 134

13.6 Application Techniques . . . 134

13.6.1 Stay Organized 135
13.6.2 Explore Ideal Candidacy 135
13.6.3 Tailor Your Approach 137
13.6.4 Evaluate Your Experience 137
13.6.5 Prove Yourself through Essays 138
13.6.6 Ace Your Interview 140

Chapter 1

GMAT and Its Relevance

1.1 Overview of GMAT

Business School applicants, depending on admissions criteria, are usually required to take the Graduate Management Admissions Test (GMAT). Unlike academic grades, which have varying significance based on each school's grading guidelines, the GMAT scores are based on the same standard for all test takers and they help business schools assess the qualification of an individual against a large pool of applicants with diverse personal and professional backgrounds. The GMAT scores play a significant role in admissions decisions since they are more recent than most academic transcripts of an applicant and they evaluate a person's verbal, quantitative and writing skills.

The GMAT is a 4-hour Computer Adaptive Test (CAT) and can be taken at any one of many test centers around the world 5 or 6 days a week. The GMAT consists of four separately timed sections. Each of the first two 30-minute sections consists of an analytical writing task, also known as Analytical Writing Assessment (AWA). The remaining two 75-minute sections (Quantitative and Verbal) consist of multiple-choice questions delivered in a computer-adaptive format. Questions in these sections are dynamically selected as you take the test to stay commensurate with your ability level. Therefore, your test will be unique. Just one question is shown on the screen at a given time. It is impossible to skip a question or go back to a prior question. Each problem needs to be answered before the next question.

You may take the GMAT only once every 31 days and no more than five times within any 12-month period. The retest policy applies even if you cancel your score within that time period. All of your scores and cancellations within the last five years will be reported to the institutions you designate as score recipients. You will receive an unofficial copy of your scores immediately after completing the exam and prior to leaving the testing center. Your official score report will be available to you on-line via an email notification 20 days after test day. Paper score report will be available via mail upon request only.

2006 has ushered in a wave of changes in the administration process (not the actual test content) of the GMAT. This is a result of the General Management Admission Council (GMAC)'s decision to switch from its previous test administrator ETS (Educational Testing Service) to Pearson VUE, the electronic testing business of Pearson. There have not been any test content changes. Rather, some logistics have been revised and improved, such as the replacement of scratch paper with erasable laminated graph paper and the requirement of completing the AWA sections before proceeding to the Quantitative and Verbal sections.

The scores necessary to get into top schools are increasing year by year. Studies indicate that applicants who prepare for the GMAT score substantially higher than those who don't. In addition to the admissions process, GMAT scores are also considered in job recruitments and scholarship awards. A good GMAT score can save you thousands of dollars in tuition. Disciplined and dedicated preparation for the GMAT will allow you to get the best score possible on the exam and get into the school of your choice.

1.2 GMAT Scores and Sections

Total GMAT scores range from 200 to 800. About 66% of test takers score between 400 and 600. The Verbal and Quantitative scores range from 0 to 60. The Verbal and Quantitative scores measure different things and cannot be compared to each other, however, each section's score can be compared across different GMAT tests. Scaled scores of 750 out of 800 on the combined test generally correspond to the 99th percentile. 680 out of 800 corresponds to the 90th percentile.

There are two categories in the Quantitative Section with 37 questions in total: Problem Solving and Data Sufficiency. The Verbal Section is comprised of three groups with 41 questions in total: Sentence Correction, Critical Reasoning, and Reading Comprehension. In both the Quantitative and Verbal sections, everyone starts out with an average difficulty level. For each correct answer you give, you are given a harder question for each subsequent question and for each incorrect answer you are given an easier question. This process will continue until you finish the section, at which point the computer will have an accurate assessment of your ability level in that subject area. In each section, all test categories can appear in a random order and a mixed manner. Your score is determined by three factors: 1) the number of questions you complete; 2) the number of questions you answer correctly and; 3) the level of difficulty and other statistical characteristics of each question. To derive a final score, these questions are weighted based on their difficulty and other statistical properties, not their position in the test. For the AWA section, one person and one computer programmed for grading (E-rater) score each essay based on essay content, organization, grammar and syntactic variety. Graders assign scores out of 6.0 based on intervals of 0.5 points. Your final, single score is an average of both individual scores obtained on the issue and argument essays. AWA scores are computed separately from other sections and have no effect on the Verbal, Quantitative, or Total scores.

1.3 GMAT Preparation and Test-taking Logistics

High quality preparation is essential to achieving your best score on the GMAT. High quality preparation means becoming intimately acquainted with the test structure, format, and the types of questions that are being asked. It means improving upon your weak areas through practice and repetition. It means developing your ability to answer correctly the tougher questions. It also means becoming aware of the types of answers that tend to be the correct ones.

Are there any advantages of taking a top-quality GMAT Prep course versus studying alone with the books and CDs available on the market? It really depends on your academic background, study habits, availability and, ultimately, your desired test score. Preparing on your own can save you some financial resources, but may not be as effective as learning from instructors who dissect each answer and impart knowledge and advice from their own GMAT-taking and MBA experiences. Studies show that visualization and discussion in a seminar environment will enable you to recognize complex structures better than learning the same material in a non-interactive way.

When setting a test date and look up test centers at http://www.mba.com/mba/TaketheGMAT, keep in mind the following: 1) Consider the times of day you tend to be able to concentrate best. Take your test in the morning or afternoon accordingly. 2) Make sure the week before your test day will not be a stressful one. This will help you concentrate, be well rested, calm and in the right frame of mind to ace the GMAT. 3) Be aware of application deadlines and do your best to provide yourself with enough time after the exam to focus on the other parts of your Business School applications.

The fee to take the GMAT is U.S. $250 worldwide. The fee for rescheduling the date, time, or location of the test is US$50 for each appointment you change. When you want to reschedule the GMAT, to avoid the forfeiture of your test fee, you must allow at least 7 calendar days between the day you reschedule your appointment and your test day. On your test day, you may select up to five schools to receive your scores before you take the test. Once you have made your selection, you will not be able to change or delete the list of schools. If you would like to send your scores to more schools, you may order additional score reports, at a cost of U.S. $28 per school. Your unofficial score report containing Total score and Quantitative and Verbal section scores is available upon your completion of the test. The only opportunity that you will have to cancel your scores is immediately after you complete the test, but before you view your scores. You cannot cancel your scores after they are displayed or reported to you.

1.4 Quantitative Section

You'll have 75 minutes to answer 37 quantitative questions after completing one hour of essays and a 5-minute break. Out of 37 quantitative questions, 23-24 are Problem Solving questions, the remaining 13-14 questions are Data Sufficiency.

Please note that not all of the quantitative questions are scored. Approximately 33 of the 37 questions are scored. The un-scored questions are there for the purpose of gauging results for future tests.

The Quantitative section measures your basic mathematical skills, understanding of elementary concepts, and the ability to reason quantitatively, solve quantitative problems, and interpret graphic data. Problem Solving and Data Sufficiency questions are intermingled throughout the section.

The rough distribution of quantitative questions is the following:

- 65% - Arithmetic (Including Statistics, probability and combinatorics)
- 25% - Algebra
- 10% - Geometry

Basic Concepts:

- Integers and Prime numbers
- Fractions and Percentages
- Mark-up and Margin
- Exponents and Roots
- Equations and Inequalities
- Probability, Permutations and Combinations
- Statistics, Graph and Data Interpretation
- Coordinate Geometry, Area and Volume of Various Geometrical Objects
- Others to Be Discussed in Class

Major Question Types:

- Solving Equations
- Profit, Cost and Break-Even Calculations
- Distance-Rate-Time Problems
- Divisibility
- Averages and Weighted Averages
- Word Problems
- Data and Graph Interpretation
- Area and Volume of Geometrical Shapes
- Mixture Problems
- Others to Be Discussed in Class

1.5 Key Preparation and Test-taking Strategies

During your GMAT preparation, be sure to incorporate the following approaches:

- Ascertain your preferred and most effective learning style (accelerated timeline vs. steady progress; controlled vs. self-paced study environment; studying in groups vs. individually; classroom learning vs. one-on-one private tutoring)
- Manage your test anxiety. Minimize your worries and pay attention to good nutrition and adequate exercise. Maintain adequate sleep with a consistent schedule leading up to your test.
- Make a special effort to improve your weaknesses along with strengthening your expertise during practice.

During the weeks and days before the test:

- Take a few days off work right before the test. Depending on your own test-taking and learning style, either relax completely or do one practice test at your scheduled test time each day. Then review the result and relax for the remainder of the day. You may want to take the day before the test off entirely so that your brain can relax more right before the test day. Be sure not to over-study the day before the test.
- Memorize the most typical problems and answer types.
- Review all prior mistakes along with explanations.
- Make a list of those typical errors you tend to make and consciously remind yourself of them and refrain from making the same mistakes.
- Save the free GMATPrep software from www.mba.com for right before the actual test and practice the tests in a mock test setting of your choice so that your memory of the actual question types and difficulty levels which have appeared in prior GMAT tests stays fresh.

When you are ready to take the practice CATs, **we recommend**:

- Create a study environment that is as similar as possible to the actual testing setting, which typically includes a quiet space, possibly a computer room or office environment. For example, locate or set up a serious test-taking environment in your house or a public library or a park or another facility so that you can exclusively focus on taking the mock tests.
- Use a systematic approach to your test. Take all questions seriously and answer them. Skipping questions is not helpful on the GMAT CAT.
- Do not take prolonged breaks during a practice test. In the actual test center, you will not be allowed coffee breaks etc. during sections. There is only one 5-minute break after the 60-minute AWA section and another 5-minute break after the 75-minute Quantitative section.
- Eliminate distractions and be conscious of time. Especially when you taking practice tests, be as aware of the clock as you will need to be on the actual exam.
- After completing a practice test, be sure to go over the questions you answered incorrectly. This is the only way to improve. You must understand your mistakes so that you will not make them on the test. (Manhattan Review provides you with over 100 pages of detailed solution guides!)
- AND practice, practice, practice!

Remember that the actual exam is on the computer so take advantage of opportunities to practice with Computer Adapted Tests. For many test-takers, reading large amounts of material on the screen is not easy. It not only dries out their eyes but also makes it hard to absorb the material. Simply practice reading etc. on the computer. The only way to improve is to practice, but be sure to practice with the right approach in a smart and effective way.

When scheduling your test, please remember to select:

- The best possible time of day for you
- A low stress week
- AND give yourself sufficient time to prepare fully for the test

In addition, **we recommend** a few general GMAT taking strategies:

On the day of the test:

- Keep a light-hearted and positive attitude on the test day.
- Bring something warm to put on in case the room is too cold. According to test center rules, you have to wear the sweater or coat instead of just putting it around your shoulders. So make sure that the additional layer of sweater or coat is comfortable in a test-taking setting.
- Also be sure you can remove a layer of clothing in case the room is hot.
- Bring something light to drink or eat such as a small piece of chocolate or protein bar. A bottle of water or a soft drink with a cap is preferred over a can so that you can minimize the chances of spilling. (Though you can not take anything into the testing room, you will be assigned a small locker. During your 5-minute breaks, you can have a few sips to stay hydrated or a bite to eat if you get hungry. Normally test centers allow you to put it outside on a desk or at an easily reachable spot or inside your locker so that you can quickly grab the drink or the food.)
- No testing aids such as study notes, calculators and PDAs are allowed. Normally 1 booklet of 10 pages of yellow laminated graph paper will be provided.
- Bring earplugs if you feel comfortable with using them to stay focused.
- Follow your normal routine.
- Arrive at the test at least 30 minutes early.

At the test:

- Do concentrate on the first 10 questions of each section most. At the beginning of each section, the total number of questions and the total time allowed are stated.
- Guess and estimate when necessary.
- Do not panic. Focus on one question at a time. Focus on one section at a time. Do not think beyond your current section and lose your concentration.
- Do not get fixated and spend unreasonable time on any single question. It will not make or break your score. Because the score per section is partially based on the number of questions you answer, try to answer as many questions as you can.
- Do not leave any questions unanswered before the section time runs out. Always submit an answer after some educated or blind guesses. Remember that you cannot skip questions or change an answer once you confirm it.

- If a few questions or passages are difficult to understand, do not let that prompt you to cancel your score entirely. You never know.
- If something is wrong with the computer, or if someone is bothering you, or if it's miserably hot etc., signal to an exam proctor. The proctor walks around in the test room every 15-20 minutes.
- Pace yourself and keep track of your progress by checking the amount of time you have left on the test screen. Each section is 75 minutes. You have about two minutes per Quantitative question and about 1.75 minutes per Verbal question.
- Pay attention to the number of questions that remain in a section. There are 37 quantitative section questions. There are 41 verbal section questions.
- Clicking on "HELP" or hiding the "TIME" information doesn't pause or stop the time.
- Between test sections, replenish your supply of laminated graph paper.
- Take advantage of breaks. Rest your eyes, as the computer screen is difficult to stare at for 4 hours straight.
- Maintain a focused mind and a positive winning attitude throughout the entire test. Remember the final problems can sometimes be equally as important as the initial ones.
- Answer all questions on the test!

Student Notes:

Chapter 2

Key Glossary

Note: This extensive glossary includes major math terms, which may go beyond the GMAT requirements. Please study it at your own discretion.

2.1 Arithmetic

Absolute Value — The numerical value of a number without taking into consideration whether the number is either positive or negative.

Addend — The number to be added.

Addition — The operation of summing two or more numbers.

Additive Inverse — The opposite of a number. The sum of any number and its additive inverse is 0.

Approximation — An estimate of an amount that could be either slightly higher or lower than the true value of the amount. Related phrases include Approximate Number, Approximate Solution and Approximate Value.

Braces — Grouping symbols { } used to include brackets. Also used to represent a set.

Brackets — Grouping symbols [ ] used to include parentheses.

Canceling — Dividing both a numerator and a denominator by the same number.

Cardinal number — A number used to indicate a quantity, not the order, e.g. 5 or 15.

Carry — Add the excess number over 10 onto the next digit when adding numbers.

Circulating decimal — A decimal number in which the digits after the decimal point repeat indefinitely. Also known as Decimal with Recurring Digits, e.g. 3.1212... or 8.4444...

Common Denominator — A number that can be divided by all denominators involved in a calculation.

Common Factors — Factors which are the same for two or more numbers.

Common Multiples — Multiples which are the same for two or more numbers.

Complex Fraction — A fraction having a fraction or fractions in the numerator and/or denominator.

Composite Number — A number divisible by more than just 1 and itself (e.g. 4, 8, 9). 0 and 1 are not composite numbers.

Consecutive Numbers — Number next to each other in a sequence, e.g., 1, 2, 3, 4, etc. Consecutive odd numbers are 1, 3, 5, 7, 9, etc.

Cube — The result when a number is multiplied twice by itself.

Cube Root — The result that when multiplied twice by itself gives you the original number, e.g., 5 is the cube root of 125, i.e. $\sqrt[3]{125} = 5$

Decimal Fraction — Fraction with a denominator of 10, 100, 1,000, etc, written using a decimal point, e.g., 0.4, 0.375.

Decimal Point — A point used to distinguish decimal fractions from whole numbers.

Denominator — The part of a fraction below the fraction bar.

Difference — The result of a subtraction.

Distributive Property — The process of distributing the number outside of the parentheses to each number inside, e.g., $a(b + c) = ab + ac$.

Divisibility — The possibility of a number to be divided by specific whole numbers without remainders.

Even Number — An integer (positive whole numbers, zero, and negative whole numbers) divisible by 2 with no remainder.

Expanded Notation — Laying out the place value of a digit by writing the number as the digit times its place value, e.g., $541 = (5 \times 10^2) + (4 \times 10^1) + (1 \times 1)$.

Factor (noun) — A number or symbol which divides evenly into a larger number, e.g., 6 is a factor of 24.

Factor (verb) — To find two or more numbers or symbols whose product equals the original combination.

Factorization — To express a number as a product of its factors. Prime Factorization is to write an integer as a product of powers of prime numbers. For example, The prime factorization for 30 is $2 \times 3 \times 5$, 2001 is $3 \times 23 \times 29$.

Finite — A number is countable because it has a definite ending.

Fraction — A number that is not a whole number. Consists of a numerator and a denominator, e.g., 4/7 or 11/3.

Greatest Common Factor — The largest factor common to two or more numbers.

Hundredth — The second decimal place to the right of the decimal point, e.g., .09 is nine hundredths.

Imaginary Numbers — A number derived from taking the square root of a negative number.

Improper Fraction — A fraction in which the numerator is greater than the denominator, e.g., $\frac{5}{3}$.

Infinite — Not able to be counted because there is no end to it. Continues forever.

Integer — A whole number, either positive, negative, or zero.

Interval — All of the numbers that are contained within a certain boundary.

Invert — Turn a fraction upside down, e.g., if we invert 2/5, we get 5/2.

Irrational Number — A number that is not rational, e.g., $\sqrt{5}$ or π. It also can be written as decimals but cannot be written as a fraction x/y, with x a natural number and y an integer.

Least Common Multiple	The smallest multiple that is common to two or more numbers.
Lowest Common Denominator	The smallest number that can be divided by all denominators involved in a calculation.
Minuend	The number in the equation from which another number (subtrahend) is subtracted.
Mixed Number	A number containing both a whole number and a fraction, e.g., 41/5.
Multiples	Numbers that are divided equally by other smaller integers, such as 2, 3, 4, etc.
Multiplicand	The number to be multiplied with.
Multiplicative Inverse	The reciprocal of a number. If you multiply any number and its multiplicative inverse, the result is 1.
Multiplier	The number used to multiple with multiplicand. Multiplicator.
Natural Number	Any positive counting number, such as 1, 2, 3, etc. Depending on the definition, Natural Numbers can include 0.
Negative Number	A number whose value is less than zero.
Number Line	A line that shows where the positive and negative numbers are in relation to zero. The positive numbers are placed to the right of the zero and the negative numbers are placed to the left of the zero.
Number Series	Numbers that are arranged in a specific predictable pattern.
Numerator	The number or symbol that is placed on top of the bar in a fraction.
Odd Number	A whole number that is not evenly divisible by 2, i.e., there is a remainder left, such as 11.
Operation	Refers to basic arithmetic operations such as multiplication, addition, subtraction, or division.
Operand	The entity to which a mathematical operation is performed on.
Order of Operations	The order in which operations are performed, e.g., multiplication is performed before addition. Addition can be performed at the same time with subtraction.
Ordinal number	Numerical words that show the position of a number, such as first, second, third.
Parentheses	Grouping symbols. ( )
Percentage	A proportion that is calculated by multiplying a fraction by 100, e.g., 87% is $\frac{87}{100}$.
Periodic Decimal	Indicates a decimal fraction in which the sequence of digits to the right of the decimal point is endlessly repeated. Also known as Recurring Decimal.
Place Value	The value assigned to a digit based on its position in a number, e.g., the place value of 5 in 51 is 10.
Positive Number	A number greater than zero.
Prime Number	A number that can only by divided by itself and 1. It will give a remainder if divided by any other number. Prime numbers include 2, 3, 5, 7 etc. Please note that 0 and 1 are not prime.
Product	The result of the multiplication of two or more things.
Proper Fraction	A fraction in which the denomination is greater than the numerator, e.g., 4/5.
Proportion	Expressed as two ratios that are equal to each other, e.g., 5 is to 3 as 10 is to 6, or 5/3 = 10/6.
Quotient	The result of the division of two numbers.
Ratio	A comparison between two numbers which is the same as dividing one number by the other. It may be expressed as x:y, x/y, or x is to y.
Rational Number	An integer or fraction such as 1, or 9/5 or 5/8. Any number that can be written as a fraction x/y with x and y being integers. Examples of irrational numbers include $\sqrt{5}$ or π. The term "rational" comes from the word "ratio". 0 is a rational number.
Real Number	A number that is either rational or irrational. The set of real numbers is also called the continuum. The real numbers can be extended with the addition of the imaginary number i, equal to $\sqrt{-1}$.
Reciprocal	The multiplicative inverse of a number. If you multiply a number with its reciprocal (multiplicative inverse), the result is 1, e.g., 7/2 is the reciprocal of 2/7
Reduce	To express a fraction in its lowest terms.
Reducing	Simply a fraction into its lowest terms, e.g., 2/6 is reduced to 1/3.
Rounding Off	Approximating a number by changing it to a nearest place value. For example, if we round off 52, it is 50. If we round off 21.7, it is 22.
Scientific Notation	A short-hand way of expressing very large or small numbers by multiplying a number between 1 and 10 by a power of 10, e.g., 3.5×10^7.
Subtrahend	A number to be subtracted.
Sum	The result of adding numbers together.
Tenth	The first number that is written to the right of the decimal point. For example, .9 is ninth tenths.
Terminate	To come to an end.

Terminating Decimal	A non-repeating decimal because it has a definite end.
Unknown	A variable whose value is not determined.
Value	The numerical quantity given to a variable.
Whole Number	A positive or negative number, including zero. Other examples include -5, 1, 2, 3, etc. Whole numbers do not contain fractions or decimal points. Also known as Integer.

2.2 Algebra

Algebra	A specific area of mathematics in which symbols represent unknown numbers and equations are consisted of various operations. Relevant phrases: Algebraic Curve, Algebraic Equation, Algebraic Expression, Algebraic Form, Algebraic Identity, Algebraic Operation, Algebraic Product, Algebraic Set, Algebraic Symbol, Algebraic Term, Algebraic Value, Algebraic Product.
Algebraic Fractions	Fractions that use variables in either the numerator or denominator, or both.
Ascending Order	Arranging numbers or terms so that each successive number or term is greater than the previous one.
Axiom	A fundamental proposition that is assumed to be true and is used to prove other propositions.
Binomial	An algebraic expression that is made up of two terms.
Binomial Coefficient	The number placed in front of the variable in a two-part mathematical expression. For example, the numbers 4 and 5 in the expression $4x - 5y$.
Binomial Equation	A mathematical expression made up of two terms and a plus or minus sign.
Closed Interval	An interval which includes two fixed boundaries or endpoints.
Coefficient	The number that is placed in front of a variable. For example, in $9x$, 9 is the coefficient.
Constant	A fixed value. Related terms include Constant Coefficient, Constant Factor and Constant Term.
Converse	The opposite of something.
Convert	To change from one system of measurement to another system.
Cross-multiplication	A multiplication method in which the opposite ends multiply each other to get the product.
Degree of Polynomial	The highest power to which a variable in the polynomial is raised.
Dissimilar Term	Terms that are different from one another.
Descending Order	Expressing the terms sequentially in decreasing order; the first term expressed will be of the highest value and then the sequential terms will be of lesser value.
Equation	A mathematical sentence in which there is a balanced relationship between the numbers and or symbols.
Evaluate	To determine the numerical amount or value of something.
Exponent	A positive or negative number placed next to a number on the upper-right corner. Expresses the power to which the quantity is to be raised or lowered.
Extremes	The outermost terms in a set of numbers. Outer terms.
Extract a Root	To calculate the root of a number in a radical sign.
Factorization of Algebraic Equations	A factored form of a polynomial in which each factor is a linear polynomial. For example, a factorization of $2y^3 – 6y^2 + 4y$ is $2y(y – 1)(y – 2)$.
F.O.I.L. Method	A multiplication method for binomials in which the first terms are multiplied first, then the outside terms, then the inside terms, and the last terms are multiplied last. Mnemonic for multiplying 2 binomials$(x + y)(x + y)$: F - First Terms: $x \cdot x$; O - Outside Terms: $x \cdot y$; I - Inside Terms: $y \cdot x$; L - Last Terms: $y \cdot y$
Fractional Equation	An equation that contains a rational expression on either sides or both sides of the equal sign.
Fractional Exponent	Using rational numbers as exponents. The integer exponent is used in the numerator and the denominator is the root. Rule: $a^{m/n} = \sqrt[n]{a^m}$ or $(\sqrt[n]{a})^m$. Examples: $5^{2/3} = \sqrt[3]{5^2} = \sqrt[3]{25}, 16^{5/4} = (\sqrt[4]{16})^5 = 2^5 = 32$.
Half-Open Interval	An interval that has only one fixed point and the other is open.
Incomplete Quadratic Equation	A quadratic equation in which a term is missing.
Inequality	A mathematical statement in which the relationships between the numbers and or variables are not equal. The opposite of an equation.
Integral	The integral of a function. A definite integral is written $\int_a^b f(x)dx$. An indefinite integral is written without any numbers such as "a" and "b" next to the integral sign.
Leading Coefficient	The number in a polynomial that has the variable that is raised to the highest degree. For example, 7 is the leading coefficient of $7x^4 – 6x^3 + 4x – 12$.
Like Term	Terms which have the same variables and corresponding powers and/or roots. Like terms can be combined using addition and subtraction. Terms that are not like cannot be combined using addition or subtraction. Example: $6x^2y$ and $7x^2y$ are like terms.
Linear Equation	When plotted on a coordinate plane, the solution to this equation forms a straight line.

Literal Equation	An equation that is mostly made up of variables.
Monomial	An algebraic mathematical expression that is made up of only one term.
Nonlinear Equation	When plotted on a coordinate plane, the solution of the equation does not form a straight line.
Open Interval	An interval that does not contain endpoints.
Polynomial	An algebraic expression made up of two terms and a positive or negative sign.
Power	The number of times in which a number must be multiplied by itself. The power is written above the base number to be multiplied by itself. For example, $5 \times 5 \times 5 = 5^3$, read "five to the third power" or "the third power of five." Power and exponent are sometimes used interchangeably.
Proper Fraction	A fraction in which the denomination is greater than the numerator.
Quadratic Equation	An equation that includes second degree polynomials and could be written as $Ax^2 + Bx + C = 0$.
Radical Sign	A symbol used to indicate square or higher roots.
Radicand	The number under the radical sign from which a square root is derived.
Reduced Equation	An equation whose terms have been simplified to their lowest terms.
Solution Set or Solution	Includes all of the solutions to the equation.
Square	The outcome of multiplying a number by itself. Perfect square is the square of a rational number. For example, 4, 9, 25, $\frac{1}{25}$ and $\frac{9}{4}$. Likewise, imperfect square is the square of an irrational number. For example, 13, 28 and $\frac{17}{3}$.
Square Root	Also called a radical or Surd. If x is a square root of y, then $x^2 = y$, or $x = \sqrt{y}$. 5 is the square root of 25. Its symbol is $\sqrt{25} = 5$.
System of Equations	Two or more equations that have common variables.
Term	An expression, either numerical or literal, that has its own sign.
Theorem	A mathematical formula or proposition that is able to be proved.
Trinomial	An algebraic expression that is made up of three terms.
Variable	A symbol that is used to represent a number.

2.3 Geometry

Acute Angle	An angle which measures less than 90°.
Acute Triangle	A triangle whose angles are all acute.
Adjacent Angles	Two angles that share a common vertex and a common side. These angles do not overlap each other.
Alternate Angle	Either alternate exterior or alternate interior angles.
Alternate Exterior Angle	Two exterior angles that are located on opposite sides of a transversal which lie on different parallel lines.
Alternate Interior Angle	Two interior angles which are located on different parallel lines and on opposite sides of the transverse line.
Altitude	The perpendicular distance from the vertex of a triangle to its base.
Altitude of a Triangle	The distance between the vertex of the triangle and its opposite side
Angle	Created by two rays which share a common end point. Angles are either measured in degrees or radians. Relevant phrases include Angle of a Circular Segment, Angle of a Circumference, Angle of Contingence, Angle of Incidence, Angle of Inclination, Angel of Intersection, and Angle of Parallelism.
Angle of Depression	The angle below the horizontal that the observer must look at in order to see whether the object is lower than the observer. Note: The angle of depression is congruent to the angle of elevation.
Angle of Elevation	The angle above the horizontal that the observer must look at in order to see if the object is higher than the observer. Note: The angle of elevation is congruent to the angle of depression.
Angular Bisector	A line or ray that will divide an angle into two equal parts. For polygons, an angle bisector is a line that bisects an interior angle.
Arc	A group of points that are located in the interior of a central angle in a circle.
Area	The space located within a specific shape. The units of measurement for area are square units.
Axis of Symmetry	The line on a graph that creates symmetry for that graph. The sides of the graph on either sides of the axis of symmetry that look identical to one another; they are mirror images of each other.
Bar	A line, such as the division line in a fraction.
Base	The bottom of a figure in a plane or solid geometry. When referring to a trapezoid, the top and bottom sides of the trapezoid that are parallel to each other are both bases. Relevant phrases include Base Angle, Base Line.
Bisect	Dividing something into two equal parts.
Bisector of an Angle	A line segment that divides the angle into two equal halves.
Central Angle	An angle in a circle who uses the center of the circle as its vertex.
Center of a Circle	The center point in a circle.
Chord	A line segment in the interior of the circle that is used to join any two points on a circle.
Circle	Located within a plane, it is the set of points which are all located equidistant from a given point.
Circumcenter	Found at the point of intersection of the perpendicular bisectors of the sides. It is the center of the circumcircle. For any circumscribable polygon, the circumcenter is found at the point of intersection of the perpendicular bisectors of the sides.
Circumcircle	A circle that goes through all of the vertices of a plane figure. It has the entire figure in its interior.
Circumference	The measurement of the distance around a circle. Calculated using either 2π multiplied by the radius or π multiplied by the diameter of the circle.
Circumradius	The radius of a cicumcircle.
Circumscribed	To enclose one figure within another geometrical shape.
Circumscribed circle	A circle that goes through all of the vertices of a plane figure. It has the entire figure in its interior. Same as Circumcircle.
Complementary Angles	Two angles whose sum will measure 90°.
Concave	A shape or solid with an indentation or "cave". A geometric figure is concave if there is at least one line segment connecting interior points which passes outside of the figure. Non-convex.
Concentric Circles	Circles that each has the same center.
Cone	A three dimensional pointed figure created by straight lines through a vertex to the points of a fixed curve.
Congruent	Equal in size and shape.
Congruent Squares	Squares which are equal in shape.
Congruent Triangles	Triangles that are equal in shape and therefore have equal angles.

Consecutive Angles	Two angles right next to each other.
Convex	A geometric figure with no indentations. A geometric figure is convex if every line segment connecting interior points is entirely contained within the figure's interior. Non-concave.
Corresponding	Being in identical positions.
Cube	A six sided solid object whose sides are equally shaped squares.
Decagon	A plane closed geometric figure that is made up of ten sides and ten angles.
Degree	The unit used to measure an angle.
Diagonal of a Polygon	A line segment that connects two vertices that are located on opposite sides of each other.
Diameter	A line segment, or chord, that has its endpoints on the circle and it must pass through the center of the circle.
Edge	The line of a figure where two faces of the figure meet each other.
Ellipse	A shape that looks like an oval.
Equiangular Polygon	A multi-sided figure, a polygon, that has equal angles
Equilateral Triangle	A triangle in which all of the sides and angles are equal.
Exterior Angle	An angle that is created by extending one side of a polygon. In a triangle, the measure of an exterior angle equals the sum of the measures of the two remote interior angles.
Face	The plane surface or side of a geometric object.
Height	The altitude of a geometric figure. From the highest point, a perpendicular line drawn to the base.
Heptagon	A plane closed geometric figure made up of seven sides and seven angles.
Hexagon	A plane closed geometric figure made up of six sides and six angles.
Hypotenuse	In a right triangle, the side opposite the 90° angle.
Incongruent	Not equal in size and shape.
Inscribed Angle	An angle formed by two chords within a circle. Its vertex is on the circle. The measure of an inscribed angle equals one-half the measure of its arc. Relevant phrases: Inscribed Circle, Inscribed Triangle.
Interior Angles	The angles created inside a shape or within two parallel lines.
Intersecting Lines	Lines that connect at a certain point.
Isosceles Right Triangle	A triangle that has one 90°, two equal sides, and two equal angles.
Isosceles Triangle	A triangle that has two equal sides and two equal angles.
Legs	In a right triangle, the two sides forming the 90° angle. In a trapezoid, the two nonparallel sides.
Line Segment	A piece of a line that has two endpoints.
Lozenge	A diamond-shaped figure.
Median	In a triangle, a line segment drawn from a vertex to the midpoint of the base. In a trapezoid, a line segment parallel to the bases and bisecting the legs.
Midpoint	A point on a line segment that is the same distance from each endpoint.
Minute	A section of an angle that is equal to one-sixtieth of a degree.
Nonagon	A plane closed geometric figure that is made up of nine sides and nine angles.
Oblique	Neither perpendicular nor parallel to another line or plane
Oblong	Having an elongated shape in which the length is greater than the width.
Obtuse Angle	An angle that measures greater than 90° and less than 180°.
Obtuse Triangle	A triangle that has one obtuse angle.
Octagon	A plane closed geometric figure made up of eight sides and eight angles.
Oval	A figure that is shaped like an elliptical, or a stretched out circle.
Parallel Lines	Two or more lines that never meet and are always the same distance apart.
Parallelogram	A four-sided plane closed figure whose opposite sides are both equal and parallel.
Parallelepiped	A three-dimensional figure with all six faces being parallelograms. Just like a rectangular solid is a three-dimensional version of a rectangle.
Pentagon	A five-sided plane closed figure whose angles add up to 540°.
Perimeter	The total length of all of the sides of a polygon.
Perpendicular Lines	Two lines that intersect at right angles.
π	A constant equaling approximately 3.14 or 22/7 that is used to compute a circle's circumference.
Plane	A flat surface that extends in all directions.
Plane Figure	A two dimensional shape that only has length and width.
Plane Geometry	The study of shapes, lines, and figures on a plane.
Point	The figure formed by the intersection of two lines.

Polygon	A closed figure with many sides.
Prism	A three dimensional figure with congruent parallel bases that are both polygons.
Pythagorean Theorem	A theorem which only applies to right triangles. The sum of the square of the two legs equals the square of the hypotenuse. ($a^2 + b^2 = c^2$).
Quadrilateral	A four-sided plane closed geometric figure whose sum of the angles is equal to 360°.
Radii	The plural form of radius.
Radius	A line segment whose endpoints lie at the center of the circle and the other at one point of the circle.
Ray	A line that has one endpoint and continues forever in one direction.
Rectangle	A polygon that has opposite sides equal and parallel and it has four right angles.
Regular Polygon	A polygon that is made up of equal sides and equal angles. Relevant phrases: Rectangular Parallelepiped, Rectangular Solid.
Rhombus	A parallelogram that is made up of four equal sides.
Right Angle	An angle that measures 90°.
Right Circular Cylinder	A right cylinder whose base meets at right angles.
Right Triangle	A triangle that contains a 90° angle.
Scalene Triangle	A triangle with unequal sides.
Segment	A section of a geometric figure.
Similar	Identical in shape, but does not have the same size, rather in proportion.
Solid Geometry	The study of surface and solids in space.
Square	A four sided polygon that has four equal and parallel sides and four right angles.
Straight Angle	An angle that measures 180°. Often called a line.
Straight Line	The shortest distance between two points.
Supplementary Angles	Two angles that add up to 180°.
Surface Area	The total surface of all sides of a solid, or the total area of faces.
Tangent to A Circle	A line, line segment, or ray that touches a circle at one point.
Trapezoid	A four sided plane closed geometric figure that has one pair of parallel sides (bases).
Triangle	A three sided plane closed geometric figure. Contains three angles the sum of whose measures is 180°.
Vertex	The point at which two rays meet and form an angle, or the point at which two sides meet in a polygon. Vertical.
Vertical Angles	The formation of opposite angles by the intersection of two lines. Vertical angles are equal in measure.
Vertices	The plural of vertex.
Volume	The capacity to hold something; measured in cubic units. Volume of rectangular prism = length times width times height.

2.4 Coordinate Geometry

Abscissa	The x-coordinate in a two-dimensional system of Cartesian coordinates. For example, for the point (9, –4), the abscissa is 9.
Analytic Geometry	Using the coordinate plane to be able to study geometric figures.
Cartesian Coordinates	A mathematical system in which numbered pairs are assigned to points on a coordinate plane, such as (x, y) or (x, y, z). Commonly known as Coordinate Plane.
Coordinate Axes	Two lines in a coordinate plane which are perpendicular to each other.
Coordinate Plane	Two perpendicular number lines that create a plane in which each point on that plane is assigned a pair of numbers. The perpendicular lines are titled the x and y axis. Relevant terms include Coordinate Curves and Coordinate Function.
Cross Point	The point on a coordinate graph where two lines intersect each other.
Hyperbola	It is a conic section where there are two fixed points in which the difference between these points remains constant. The conic section can be thought of as an inside-out ellipse.
Intercept	The point where a line crosses the coordinate axis. x-intercept crosses the x-axis. y-intercept crosses the y-axis.
Open Ray	A ray that contains one fixed point and does include its endpoint (half line).
Ordered Pair	A pair of elements (x,y) which are used on a coordinate plane to either plot points or identify something.
Ordinate	Indicates the distance along the vertical axis of the coordinate graph. In other words, it is the y-coordinate in a point (x, y). For the point (9, –4), the ordinate is –4.
Origin	Has the coordinate (0,0) and is used to represent the point on the coordinate graph where the two number lines intersect each other.
Parabola	A u-shaped curve with certain specific properties. A parabola always has a quadratic equation.
Quadrants	The four division of a coordinate plane.
Rectangular Coordinates	(x,y) or (x,y,z) coordinates.
Slope	The tangent of the angle between a straight line and the x-axis.
Transversal	A line that crosses two or more parallel or nonparallel lines in a plane. Relevant phrase: Transversal Surface.
X-Axis	The horizontal axis in a coordinate graph.
X-Coordinate	The first number in the ordered pair that shows the distance on the x-axis. Abscissa.
Y-Axis	The vertical axis in a coordinate graph.
Y-Coordinate	The second number in the ordered pair that shows the distance on the y-axis. Ordinate.

2.5 Word Problems

Balance	Beginning balance is the principal in interest problems. Ending balance is the principal plus interest accrued.
Biannual	Occurring every six months. Biennial means "every two years."
Compound Interest	In interest problems, this means that the new interest is to be added to the sum of principal and the previously accrued interest at each specific interval determined by the rate. Annual rate compounds every year. Quarterly rate compounds at end of each quarter.
Dividend	In interest problems, this signifies the amount of interest paid or due.
Percentage Change	Expressed also as percent rise, percent difference, percentage increase, percentage decrease, percentage drop, etc. Found by dividing the actual amount of change by the numerical starting point.
Principal	The initial amount of money that is invested or loaned upon which interest will have to be paid.
Quarterly	Occurring every three months.
Rate	The speed at which something changes in comparison to another measured amount.
Semiannual	Occurring every six months.
Simple Interest	Interest that is applied only to the principal.
Velocity	The speed or rate at which something moves or occurs.

2.6 Statistics

Element	Any member of an ordered set.
Empty Set	A set that does not contain any numbers. Null set.
Equal Sets	Sets of numbers or variables that are identical to one another.
Equivalent Sets	Sets that have equal numbers of members in them.
Mean (Arithmetic)	The average of a set of items (total the items and divide by the number of items).
Median	The middle item in an ordered set. If the set has an even number of items, the median is the average of the two middle items.
Mode	The number appearing most frequently in a group.
Null Set	A set that is empty because it does not contain any members. Empty set.
Range	The value obtained by subtracting the smallest number from the largest number in a set of numbers.
Roster	A technique that names a set by listing every one of the members of the set.
Rule	A technique used to name a set by describing the elements within that set.
Set	A group of numbers, variables, objects, etc.
Set Builder Notation	A formal method of describing a set. Often used for inequalities. For example, $\{x\|x > 1\}$, which is read "x such that all x is greater than 1."
Subset	A set that is expressed within another set.
Universal Set	The general category set or the set of all those elements under consideration.
Weighted Mean	The mean of a group of numbers that have been multiplied by their relative importance or times of occurrence.

2.7 Combinatorics & Probability

Combinations	The total number of independent possible choices when order is irrelevant.
Dependent Events	The outcome of one event has an impact on the outcome of another event.
Independent Events	The outcome of an event has no impact on the outcome of another event.
Intersection of Sets	Members of different sets that are found in both sets.
Permutations	The total number of inter-dependent choices when order is relevant.
Probability	The numerical measure of the likelihood of the occurrence of an event.
Union of Sets	All of the numbers in a group of different sets.
Venn Diagram	A pictorial description of sets.

Student Notes:

Chapter 3

Formulae Cheatsheet

3.1 Arithmetic

(1) Number Properties

(a) Positive $\times$ Negative = Negative
(b) Negative $\times$ Negative = Positive
(c) Positive $\div$ Negative = Negative
(d) Negative $\div$ Negative = Positive

(e) Odd + Odd = Even
(f) Even + Even = Even
(g) Odd - Odd = Even
(h) Even - Even = Even
(i) Odd + Even = Odd
(j) Odd - Even = Odd

(k) Even $\times$ Odd = Even
(l) Even $\times$ Even = Even
(m) Odd $\times$ Odd $\times$ Odd $\times \ldots$ = Odd

(n) Odd $\div$ Even $\neq$ Integer
(o) Even $\div$ Odd = Even (or Fraction)
(p) Odd $\div$ Odd = Odd (or Fraction)

(2) Percentages

(a) $F = (1 + \frac{x\%}{100})I$ (F: Final Value. I: Initial Value. X: Percentage change.)
(b) % change = $\frac{F-I}{I} \times 100$

(3) Interest

(a) Simple: $R = P \times (1 + rt)$
(b) Compound: $R = P \times (1 + \frac{r}{n})^{nt}$

3.2 Algebra *

(1) Rules for Exponents

(a) $x^a \cdot x^b = x^{a+b}$

(b) $\frac{x^a}{x^b} = x^{a-b}$

(c) $x^a \cdot y^a = (xy)^a$

(d) $\left(\frac{x}{y}\right)^a = \frac{x^a}{y^a}$

(e) $(x^a)^b = x^{ab}$

(f) $x^{-a} = \frac{1}{x^a}$

(g) $x^0 = 1$, unless $x = 0$.

(h) $x^{\frac{a}{b}} = \sqrt[b]{x^a}$

(i) $\sqrt[n]{x} = x^{\frac{1}{n}}$

(2) The Quadratic Formula: $x = \frac{-b \pm \sqrt{b^2-4ac}}{2a}$

3.3 Geometry

(1) Properties of Angles

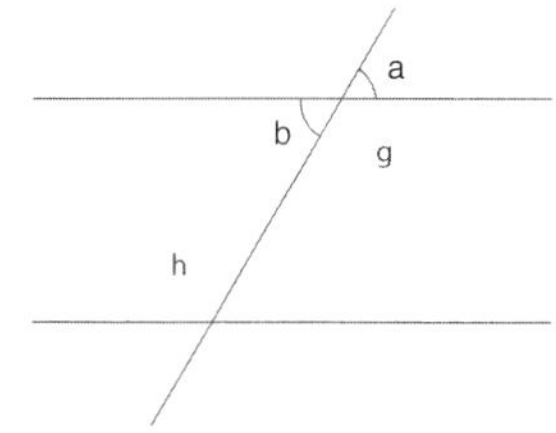

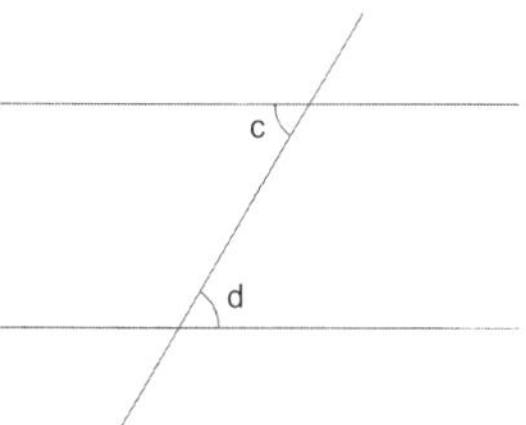

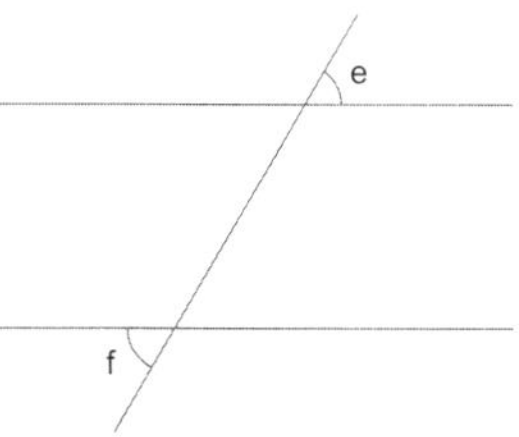

$a = b, g = h$
$a + g = 180°$
$b + h = 180°$

$c = d$

$e = f$

(2) Triangles

(a) Sum of the angles: $\angle A + \angle B + \angle C = 180°$

(b) Area of a triangle: $A = \frac{1}{2}bh$ or
Hero's Formula: $A = \sqrt{s(s-a)(s-b)(s-c)}$, where $s = \frac{a+b+c}{2}$ (Reference only. Not tested on GMAT)

(c) Relationships among sides of a triangle: $a + b > c$, $a + c > b$, and $b + c > a$

(d) Perimeter of a triangle: $P = a + b + c$

(e) Right triangles: Pythagorean Theorem $a^2 + b^2 = c^2$

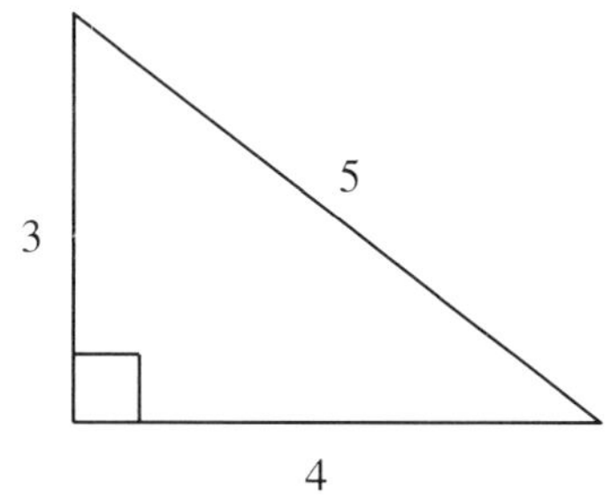

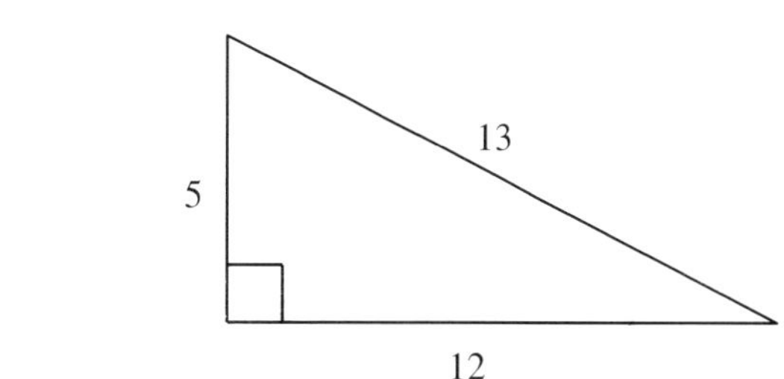

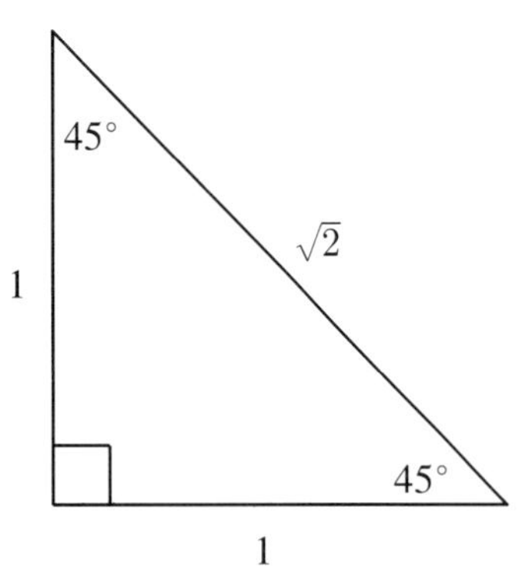

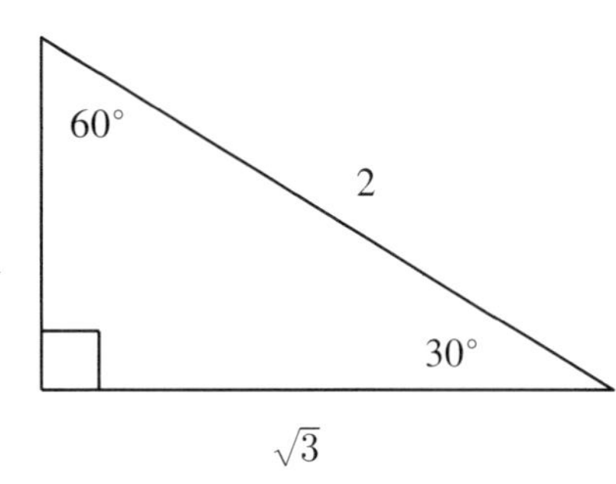

(f) Typical Right Triangle Relationships:
$1 - 1 - \sqrt{2}$ ($45° - 45° - 90°$)
$1 - \sqrt{3} - 2$ ($30° - 60° - 90°$)
$3 - 4 - 5$ / $6 - 8 - 10$
$5 - 12 - 13$ / $10 - 24 - 26$
$7 - 24 - 25$
$8 - 15 - 17$

(3) Properties of a line: $y = mx + b$

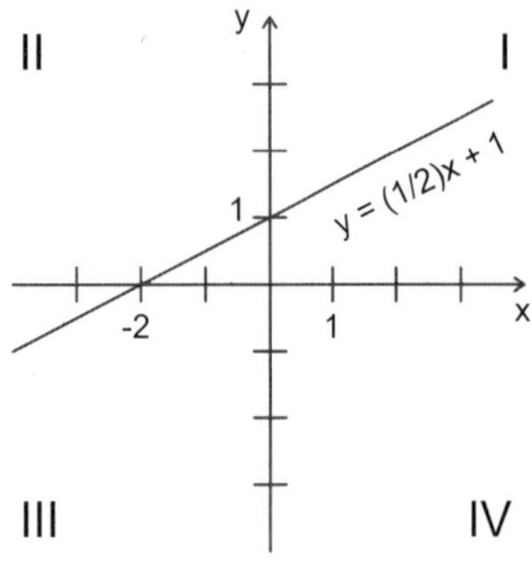

Quadrant	Value of X	Value of Y
I	+	+
II	-	+
III	-	-
IV	+	-

Properties of a line: $y = mx + b$

(a) Slope: $m = \frac{y_2 - y_1}{x_2 - x_1}$

(b) X-intercept = $-b/m$

Slope Type	Orientation
Positive	/
Negative	\
Zero	Horizontal
Undefined	Vertical

Intercept	Coordinates
x	$(x, 0)$
y	$(0, y)$

(4) Quadrilaterals

Type of Quadrilateral	Perimeter	Area	Features
Square	$4l$	l^2	All sides equal & parallel, all angles 90°, diagonal=$\sqrt{2}l$.
Rectangle	$2l + 2w$	lw	Opposite sides equal & parallel, all angles 90°
Parallelogram	$2a + 2b$	bh	Opposite sides equal & parallel, opposite angles equal
Rhombus	$2a + 2b$	$\frac{1}{2}(d \times d)$ (d - diagonal)	All sides equal, opposite angles equal, perpendicular diagona
Trapezoid	$a + b + c + d$	$\frac{1}{2}(a + c)h$	One pair of sides parallel (sides a and c)
Trapezium	$a + b + c + d$	Not easily determined	No sides parallel

Fortunately, trapezia are so difficult to work with that they very seldom appear in GMAT questions.

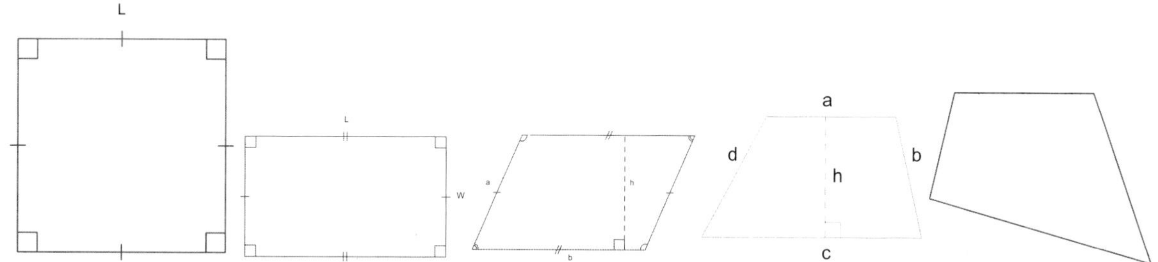

(5) Other Regular Polygons:

  (a) Measure of all angles: $(n-2)180°$

  (b) Measure of any interior angle: $\frac{n-2}{n}180°$

(6) Circles

  (a) Area: $A = \pi r^2$ ($\pi \approx \frac{22}{7}$)

  (b) Circumference: $C = 2\pi r = \pi d$

  (c) Relationship between central angle and arc: $\frac{l}{2\pi r} = \frac{\alpha}{360°}$

  (d) Area of the Sector = $\frac{\alpha}{360}\pi r^2$

  (e) Inscribed Angle = $\frac{1}{2}\times$ Central Angle

(7) Three-dimensional Figures

  (a) Cube

    i. Volume: $V = l^3$

    ii. Surface Area: $A = 6l^2$

    iii. Diagonal: $D = \sqrt{3}l$

  (b) Rectangular Solid

    i. Volume: $V = lwh$

    ii. Surface Area: $A = 2lw + 2lh + 2wh$

    iii. Diagonal: $D = \sqrt{l^2 + w^2 + h^2}$

  (c) Cylinder

    i. Volume: $V = \pi r^2 h$

    ii. Surface Area: $A = 2\pi rh + n\pi r^2, n = 0, 1, 2$

  (d) Sphere

    i. Volume: $V = \frac{4}{3}\pi r^3$

    ii. Surface Area: $A = 4\pi r^2$

3.4 Word Problems

(1) Speed Problems: $\frac{1}{t_1} + \frac{1}{t_2} = \frac{1}{t_{12}}$

(2) Rate Problems: Speed $\times$ Time = Distance

(3) Exponential Growth: $F = Ia^{n/t}$

(4) Compound Interest: Earnings = Investment $\times(1+\text{rate})^t$, t =no. of periods.

3.5 Statistics

(1) Average (Arithmetic Mean): $\bar{x} = \frac{1}{n}\sum_{i}^{n} x_i$, where x_i is the ith element of the set.

(2) Standard Deviation: $\sigma = \sqrt{\frac{\sum_{i=1}^{n}(x_i - \bar{x})^2}{n}}$

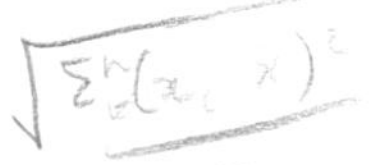

3.6 Combinatorics

(1) Permutations: ${}_nP_k = \frac{n!}{(n-k)!}$

(2) Combinations: ${}_nC_k = \frac{n!}{(n-k)!k!}$

(3) Possible circular arrangements of n items: $(n-1)!$

3.7 Probability

(1) Intersection of Two Independent Events ("And" question type): $P(A \cap B) = P(A)P(B)$

(2) Intersection of Two Dependent Events ("And" question type): $P(A \cap B) = P(A)P_A(B) = P(B)P_B(A)$

(3) Union of Two Overlapping Events ("Or" question type): $P(A \cup B) = P(A) + P(B) - P(A \cap B)$

(4) Union of Three Overlapping Events ("Or" question type): $P(A \cup B \cup C) = P(A) + P(B) + P(C) - P(A \cap B) - P(A \cap C) - P(B \cap C) + P(A \cap B \cap C)$

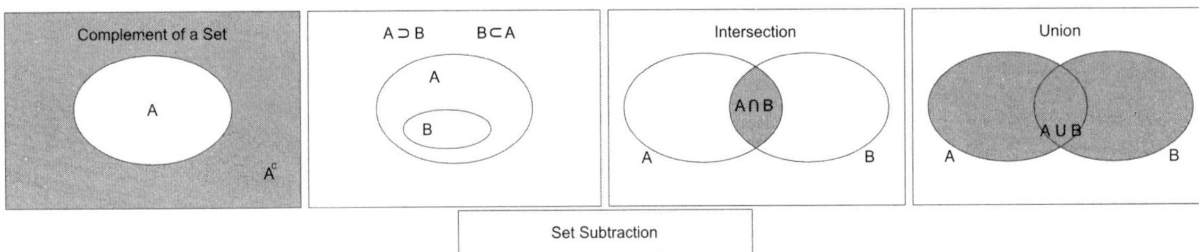

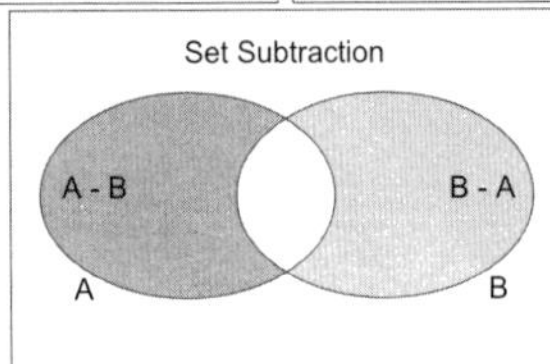

Student Notes:

Chapter 4

Quick Reference

4.1 Multiplication Table

It goes almost without saying, but we shall say it anyway, that you should know your multiplication table. During the test, you should be spending your time focusing on the crux of the problem, not that $8 \times 7 = 56$. The rote work is just that and can be done prior to the test.

	1	**2**	**3**	**4**	**5**	**6**	**7**	**8**	**9**	**10**	11	12	13	14	15
1	**1**	**2**	**3**	**4**	**5**	**6**	**7**	**8**	**9**	**10**	11	12	13	14	15
2		**4**	**6**	**8**	**10**	**12**	**14**	**16**	**18**	**20**	22	24	26	18	30
3			**9**	**12**	**15**	**18**	**21**	**24**	**27**	**30**	33	36	39	42	45
4				**16**	**20**	**24**	**28**	**32**	**36**	**40**	44	48	52	56	60
5					**25**	**30**	**35**	**40**	**45**	**50**	55	60	65	70	75
6						**36**	**42**	**48**	**54**	**60**	66	72	78	84	90
7							**49**	**56**	**63**	**70**	77	84	91	98	105
8								**64**	**72**	**80**	88	96	104	112	120
9									**81**	**90**	99	108	117	126	135
10										**100**	110	120	130	140	150
11											121	132	143	154	165
12												144	156	168	180
13													169	182	195
14														196	210
15															225

4.2 Decimals and Fractions

$$\frac{1}{4} = 0.25, \quad \frac{1}{2} = 0.5, \quad \frac{3}{4} = 0.75, \quad \frac{1}{3} = 0.33\ldots, \quad \frac{2}{3} = 0.66\ldots, \quad \frac{1}{6} = 0.166\ldots, \quad \frac{5}{6} = 0.833\ldots,$$

$$\frac{1}{8} = 0.125, \quad \frac{3}{8} = 0.375, \quad \frac{5}{8} = 0.625, \quad \frac{7}{8} = 0.875, \quad \frac{1}{9} = 0.111\ldots, \quad \frac{2}{9} = 0.222\ldots, \quad \frac{17}{20} = 0.85.$$

4.3 Squares and Square Roots

For a variety of reasons that will become clearer as you progress through the text, it is very important that you know your squares and square roots cold. Do whatever you need to do to memorize them: flash cards, electric shock therapy, etc.

$1^2 = 1$	$\sqrt{1} = 1$	$11^2 = 121$	$\sqrt{121} = 11$	$23^2 = 529$	$\sqrt{529} = 23$
$1.4^2 \cong 2$	$\sqrt{2} \cong 1.4$	$12^2 = 144$	$\sqrt{144} = 12$	$24^2 = 576$	$\sqrt{576} = 24$
$1.7^2 \cong 3$	$\sqrt{3} \cong 1.7$	$13^2 = 169$	$\sqrt{169} = 13$	$25^2 = 625$	$\sqrt{625} = 25$
$2^2 = 4$	$\sqrt{4} = 2$	$14^2 = 196$	$\sqrt{196} = 14$		
$3^2 = 9$	$\sqrt{9} = 3$	$15^2 = 225$	$\sqrt{225} = 15$		
$4^2 = 16$	$\sqrt{16} = 4$	$16^2 = 256$	$\sqrt{256} = 16$		
$5^2 = 25$	$\sqrt{25} = 5$	$17^2 = 289$	$\sqrt{289} = 17$		
$6^2 = 36$	$\sqrt{36} = 6$	$18^2 = 324$	$\sqrt{324} = 18$		
$7^2 = 49$	$\sqrt{49} = 7$	$19^2 = 361$	$\sqrt{361} = 19$		
$8^2 = 64$	$\sqrt{64} = 8$	$20^2 = 400$	$\sqrt{400} = 20$		
$9^2 = 81$	$\sqrt{81} = 9$	$21^2 = 441$	$\sqrt{441} = 21$		
$10^2 = 100$	$\sqrt{100} = 10$	$22^2 = 484$	$\sqrt{484} = 22$		

BE CAREFUL!

$(-1)^2 = 1$ but $-1^2 = -1$. Remember PEMDAS; Parentheses, Exponentiation, Multiplication, Division, Addition, and Subtraction. This is the order of operations. So exponentiation comes before multiplication.

4.4 Powers of 2 & 3

It is also very important to know your powers of 2, such as:

n	-3	-2	-1	0	1	2	3	4	5	6	7	8	9	10
2^n	1/8	1/4	1/2	1	2	4	8	16	32	64	128	256	512	1024

Powers of 3:

n	-3	-2	-1	0	1	2	3	4	5	6	7	8	9	10
3^n	1/27	1/9	1/3	1	3	9	27	81	243	729	2187	6561	19683	59049

4.5 Cubes and Cube Roots

The following factorials should also be memorized:

$1^3 = 1$	$2^3 = 8$	$3^3 = 27$	$4^3 = 64$	$5^3 = 125$
$\sqrt[3]{1} = 1$	$\sqrt[3]{8} = 2$	$\sqrt[3]{27} = 3$	$\sqrt[3]{64} = 4$	$\sqrt[3]{125} = 5$

4.6 Powers of 10

giga (G): 1,000,000,000 = 10^9
mega (M): 1,000,000 = 10^6
kilo (k): 1,000 = 10^3
hecto (h): 100 = 10^2
deka (da): = 10 = 10^1
deci (d): 0.1 = 10^{-1}
centi (c): 0.01 = 10^{-2}
milli (m): 0.001 = 10^{-3}
micro (μ): 0.000001 = 10^{-6}
nano (n): 0.000000001 = 10^{-9}

4.7 Factorials

The following factorials should also be memorized:

Factorial	Value
0!	1
1!	1
2!	2
3!	6
4!	24
5!	120
6!	720
7!	5,040

4.8 Conversions and Measurements

The following conversions are mainly for your reference. They are usually not tested in the GMAT.

4.8.1 Length

1 meter = 10 dm = 100 cm = 1000 mm
1 km = 1000 meters
1 mile = 1.61 km = 1,760 yards = 5,280 feet
1 yard = 91.44 cm
1 yard = 3 feet = 36 inches
1 foot = 12 inches = 30.48 cm
1 inch = 2.54 cm

4.8.2 Area

1 square foot (sq ft) = 144 square inches (sq in)
1 square yard (sq yd) = 9 square feet

4.8.3 Volume

1 liter = 10 dl = 10 cl = 1 cubic dm
1 cubic meter = 1000 liters
1 pint = 2 cups
1 quart = 0.95 liters = 32 ounces
1 gallon = 4 quarts = 3.79 liters

4.8.4 Mass and Weight

1 kg = 1000 g
1 kg = 2.2 pounds (lb)
1 metric ton = 1000 kg
1 lb = 16 ounces
1 g = 1000 mg

4.8.5 Temperature

Fahrenheit = $\frac{9}{5}$Celsius + 32
Celsius = $\frac{5}{9}$ (Fahrenheit - 32)

4.8.6 Approximations

A meter is a little more than a yard
A kilometer is about .621 miles
A kilogram is about 2.2 pounds
A liter is slightly more than a quart

Chapter 5

Arithmetic

5.1 Basic Concepts in Arithmetic

5.1.1 Types of Numbers

In the GMAT, one has to be familiar with the following types of numbers:

- Prime Numbers - A number that can only by divided by itself and 1. It will give a remainder if divided by any other number. Prime numbers include 2, 3, 5, 7 etc. Please note that 0 and 1 are not prime.
- Natural Numbers - Any positive counting number, such as 1, 2, 3, etc. Depending on the definition, Natural Numbers may include 0.
- Integers - A whole number, either positive, negative, or zero.
- Rational Numbers - An integer or fraction such as 1, or 9/5 or 5/8. Any number that can be written as a fraction x/y with x and y being integers. Examples of irrational numbers include $\sqrt{5}$ or π. The term "rational" comes from the word "ratio". 0 is a rational number.
- Decimals - The base-ten numeral system, which uses various symbols (called digits) for ten distinct values (0, 1, 2, 3, 4, 5, 6, 7, 8 and 9) to represent numbers.
- Real Numbers - A number that is either rational or irrational. The set of real numbers is also called the continuum. The real numbers can be extended with the addition of the imaginary number i, equal to $\sqrt{-1}$.

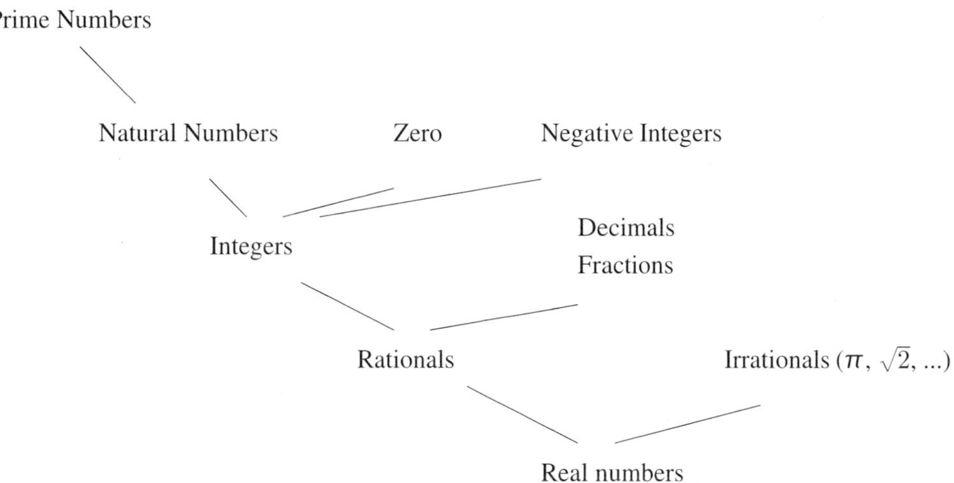

5.1.2 Fundamental Operations

Remember the following expressions while carrying out basic arithmetic operations:

- Addition: Addend + Addend = Sum
- Subtraction: Minuend - Subtrahend = Difference
- Multiplication: Factor × Factor = Product
- Division: Dividend ÷ Divisor = Quotient (If the division is perfect; otherwise...)
- Division: Dividend ÷ Divisor = Quotient + Remainder ÷ Divisor

Special Integer – 0 & 1

What is unique about 0?

Adding or subtracting 0 results in no change: $5 \pm 0 = 5$

Multiplying 0 results in 0

Dividing by 0 is invalid.

Subtracting a number from itself results in 0, e.g. 5 – 5 = 0

What is unique about 1?

Multiplying or dividing by 1 results in no change: $5 \times / \div 1 = 5$

Dividing a non-zero number by itself results in 1, e.g. $5 \div 5 = 1$

Shortcut for the Sum of Consecutive Integers

- Average the first and last term to find the middle term or point

- Derive the total number of terms
- The sum = middle point × total number of terms

$$1 + 2 + 3 + \ldots + 100 = \frac{(1+100)}{2} \times 100 = 5050$$
$$2 + 3 + 4 + \ldots + 100 = \frac{(2+100)}{2} \times [(100 - 2) + 1] = 51 \times (100 - 1) = 5049$$

Order of Operations:

Please **E**xcuse **M**y **D**ear **A**unt **S**ally.

P = Parentheses E = Exponents M = Multiplication D = Division A = Addition S = Subtraction

Sample Data Sufficiency Question

(Source: GMAT Mini-Test. Reprinted with prior permission.)

The symbol ∇ represents one of the following operations: addition, subtraction, multiplication, or division. What is the value of $3\nabla 2$?

(1) $0\nabla 1 = 1$
(2) $1\nabla 0 = 1$

○ Statement (1) ALONE is sufficient, but statement (2) alone is not sufficient.

○ Statement (2) ALONE is sufficient, but statement (1) alone is not sufficient.

○ BOTH statements TOGETHER are sufficient, but NEITHER statement ALONE is sufficient.

○ EACH statement ALONE is sufficient.

○ Statement (1) and (2) TOGETHER are NOT sufficient.

EXPLANATION:

Since $0 + 1 = 1$, $0 - 1 = -1$, $0 \times 1 = 0$, and $0 \div 1 = 0$, it follows from (1) that ∇ represents addition, so the value of $3\nabla 2$ can be determined. Hence, (1) alone is sufficient.

Since $1 + 0 = 1$, $1 - 0 = 1$, $1 \times 0 = 0$, and $1 \div 0$ is undefined, it follows from (2) that ∇ could represent either addition or subtraction, so that $3\nabla 2$ could equal 5 or 1. Thus, (2) alone is not sufficient.
The best answer is the first choice.

5.2 Number Properties

The test-taker will be expected to understand how integers behave under the operations of addition, subtraction, multiplication and division. It is necessary to recognize even, odd and prime numbers, determine the factors of a number, and manipulate positive or negative quantities.

Positive & Negative

- Multiplication or division of any two numbers with different signs will always result in a negative number. If the two numbers have the same sign, the result is always positive.

$5 \times (-2) = -10 \Rightarrow$ Positive × Negative = Negative
$\Rightarrow$ Product of two numbers with different signs is negative.

$(-5)x(-2) = 10 \Rightarrow$ Negative × Negative = Positive
$\Rightarrow$ Product of two numbers with identical signs is positive.

$12 \div (-3) = -4 \Rightarrow$ Positive ÷ Negative = Negative
$\Rightarrow$ Quotient of two numbers with different signs is negative.

$(-12) \div (-3) = 4 \Rightarrow$ Negative ÷ Negative = Positive
$\Rightarrow$ Quotient of two numbers with identical signs is positive.

Odd & Even

Addition & Subtraction

- Adding or subtracting two numbers of the same type, i.e. two even or two odd numbers, will always result in an even answer. Similarly, if the numbers are of different type, i.e. one is even and the other is odd, then the result is always an odd number. (Note that zero is an even number.)

$5 + 7 = 12 \Rightarrow$ Odd + Odd = Even
$\Rightarrow$ Sum of two odd numbers is even.

$6 + 4 = 10 \Rightarrow$ Even + Even = Even
$\Rightarrow$ Sum of two even numbers is even.

$7 - 5 = 2 \Rightarrow$ Odd - Odd = Even
$\Rightarrow$ Difference of two odd numbers is even.

$6 - 4 = 2 \Rightarrow$ Even - Even = Even
$\Rightarrow$ Difference of two even numbers is even.

$5 + 6 = 11 \Rightarrow$ Odd + Even = Odd
$\Rightarrow$ Sum of one odd and one even number is odd.

$7 - 4 = 3 \Rightarrow$ Odd - Even = Odd
$\Rightarrow$ Difference of one odd and one even number is odd.

Multiplication

- Any integer multiplied by an even integer results in an even integer. It follows therefore, that if an odd integer is created as the result of one or more multiplications, then all of the integers must have been odd.

$2 \times 7 = 14 \Rightarrow$ Even × Odd = Even
$2 \times 6 = 12 \Rightarrow$ Even × Even = Even

$\Rightarrow$ Product of an EVEN integer with any other integers is EVEN.

$7 \times 5 \times 3 = 75 \Rightarrow$ Odd × Odd × Odd × ... = Odd
$\Rightarrow$ Product of ALL odd integers is odd.

Division

- From these, the following observations concerning division of one integer by another, can be made. All such operations must be either, an odd number divided by an even number, an even number by an odd number, an even number by another even number, or an odd number divided by another odd number.

  (1) Dividing an odd number by an even number never produces an integer.

  $$9 \div 2 = 9/2 = 4\tfrac{1}{2} \Rightarrow \text{Odd} \div \text{Even} = \text{Fraction}$$

  (2) If the division of an even number by an odd number results in an integer, the resulting integer must be even.

  $$6 \div 3 = 2 \Rightarrow \text{Even} \div \text{Odd} = \text{Even}$$
  $$28 \div 7 = 4 \Rightarrow \text{Even} \div \text{Odd} = \text{Even}$$
  Or
  $$6 \div 5 = 1\tfrac{1}{5} \Rightarrow \text{Even} \div \text{Odd} = \text{Fraction}$$
  $$28 \div 9 = 3\tfrac{1}{9} \Rightarrow \text{Even} \div \text{Odd} = \text{Fraction}$$

  (3) If division of one odd number by another odd number results in an integer, that integer must be odd.

  $$15 \div 5 = 3 \Rightarrow \text{Odd} \div \text{Odd} = \text{Odd}$$
  $$21 \div 3 = 7 \Rightarrow \text{Odd} \div \text{Odd} = \text{Odd}$$
  Or
  $$15 \div 7 = 2\tfrac{1}{7} \Rightarrow \text{Odd} \div \text{Odd} = \text{Fraction}$$
  $$21 \div 5 = 4\tfrac{1}{5} \Rightarrow \text{Odd} \div \text{Odd} = \text{Fraction}$$

  (4) Simplifying by division both numerator and denominator by the largest common power of 2 will reduce the ratio to one of the three above cases.

  $$18 \div 4 = (2 \times 9) \div (2 \times 2) = 9 \div 2 = 4\tfrac{1}{2} \Rightarrow \text{Odd} \div \text{Even} = \text{Fraction}$$
  $$56 \div 14 = (2 \times 2 \times 2 \times 7) \div (2 \times 7) = 28 \div 7 = 4 \Rightarrow \text{Even} \div \text{Odd} = \text{Even}$$
  $$84 \div 12 = (4 \times 21) \div (4 \times 3) = 7 \Rightarrow \text{Odd} \div \text{Odd} = \text{Odd}$$
  $$22 \div 14 = (2 \times 11) \div (2 \times 7) = 1\tfrac{4}{7} \Rightarrow \text{Odd} \div \text{Odd} = \text{Fraction}$$

Summary

$$\text{Odd} \div \text{Even} \neq \text{Integer}$$
$$\text{Even} \div \text{Odd} = \text{Even (or Fraction)}$$
$$\text{Odd} \div \text{Odd} = \text{Odd (or Fraction)}$$

Assume you have a sum of two numbers, which are positive integers. Assume the sum is even, what can you say about the two addends?

⇒ Both even or both odd.

What can you say when the sum is odd?

⇒ One even, one odd.

Assume you have a product of two positive integers and that the product is even, what can you say about the two factors?

⇒ At least one even.

What can you say about a product of 5 numbers that is odd?

⇒ All 5 factors odd.

Student Notes:

5.2.1 Determining Factors

Working out the factors of a number is an exercise often needed for the GMAT, *e.g.* when it is necessary to simplify some given fraction. To simplify $\frac{35}{77}$, we can use a memorized multiplication table, but to attempt to simplify $\frac{91}{133}$, the problem is not so simple. In still other cases, the problem may be to determine if a particular number is divisible by some other number. There are many ways to do this. Listed in increasing order of difficulty, these are:

(1) Check by inspection.

(2) Use simplified tests of the properties of the digits.

(3) Chunking

(4) Long Division

(5) Use a computational algorithm.

5.2.2 Divisibility of Numbers

A question may require the finding of the remainder when one number is divided by another, or more specifically, working out the remainder to determine whether the divisor is a factor of the original number. When 22 is divided by 5, the result is 4 and there is a remainder of 2.

When 20 is divided by 5, the result is 4 with no remainder. In this case, 4 and 5 are called factors of 20 and you also may find the expression that 5 divides evenly in 20.

Before we discuss how to find out if a given number is divisible evenly by another number, let's discuss one special case.

What is a prime number?

⇒ Only divisible by itself and one.

Write down all prime numbers from 0 to 10.

⇒ 2, 3, 5, 7 **(not 1)**

The single most important concept in Arithmetics in the GMAT is to find out whether a number is divisible by another number.

Finding the remainder is fairly simple using the SMART (Signed Multiplication, Addition, Reduction, Technique) algorithm. Most of the following rules are SMART applications. If no remainder exists, then the divisor is a factor of the original number.

Divisibility test for **2**: last digit
Divisibility test for **3**: sum of digits
Divisibility test for **4**: last two digits
Divisibility test for **5**: last digit 0 or 5
Divisibility test for **6**: test for 2 **and** 3
Divisibility test for **7**: use **SMART** algorithm
Divisibility test for **8**: last three digits (Remember the power of 2, e.t., 64, 128, 256, 512, 1024, etc)
Divisibility test for **9**: sum of digit
Divisibility test for **11**: use **SMART** algorithm
Divisibility test for **12**: test for 3 and 4
Divisibility test for **13**: use **SMART** algorithm
Divisibility test for **14**: test for 2 and 7
Divisibility test for **15**: test for 3 and 5

(1) Divisibility by 2 or 4 or 8. If the last digit is even, the number is divisible by 2. If the last two digits are divisible by 4, so is the number. If the last 3 digits are divisible by 8, so is the number, etc. A SMART variant can be used to eliminate the need for division.

(2) Divisibility by 3 or 9. If the sum of the digits is determined and the sum is a multiple of 3 or 9 respectively, then the original number is divisible by 3 or 9 respectively. The 9's check is a SMART application.

(3) Divisibility by 5 or 25. If the last digit of a number is either 0 or 5, then the original number is divisible by 5. If in addition, the last two digits are 00, 25, 50, or 75, then the original number is divisible by 25.

(4) Divisibility by 7 is checked using the SMART algorithm.

(5) The check for divisibility by 11 requires two digit-sums. The first is obtained by adding together every other digit in the original number. The second sum is obtained by adding together all digits ignored in obtaining the first sum. If the difference of the two sums is any multiple of 11, then the original sum was divisible by 11 as well. This is also an application of the SMART algorithm.

Is the number 141922 divisible by 11?

To answer that question, subtract the sum of the odd digits of the number from the sum of the even digits of the number. If the resulting number is divisible by 11, then the original number is also divisible by 11.

```
 4+9+2  =  15
 |  |  |
141922      -
|  |  |
1+1+2  =   4
          ----
           11
```

Since 11 is divisible by 11, then 141922 is also divisible by 11.

(6) The SMART algorithm is most powerful in obtaining remainders resulting from division by the primes 13, 17 and 19. It is possible to use this procedure for division by non-prime numbers although it may be easier to use multiple checks of the factors of the non-prime divisor. Trying to use SMART for numbers greater than 19 tends to be cumbersome.

(7) If a number has a divisor, then the original number is divisible by all factors of that divisor, e.g. a number divisible by 15 must also be divisible by both 3 and 5. The converse is true only if the factors are independent, e.g., a number divisible by 3 and 5 must be divisible by 15, but a number divisible by 8 (and 4 and 2) is not necessarily by 16.

Student Notes:

5.2.3 Chunking

Another way to check divisibility is to reduce the number in chunks. For example, is 532 divisible by 11? You know that 44 is divisible by 11 and therefore so is 440. That leaves 92, which is easily seen not to be divisible by 11.

5.2.4 Long Division

Another way to find a remainder of division is to use *long division*.

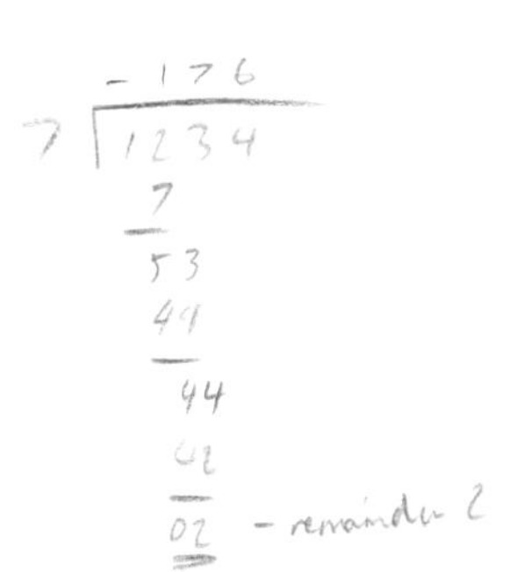

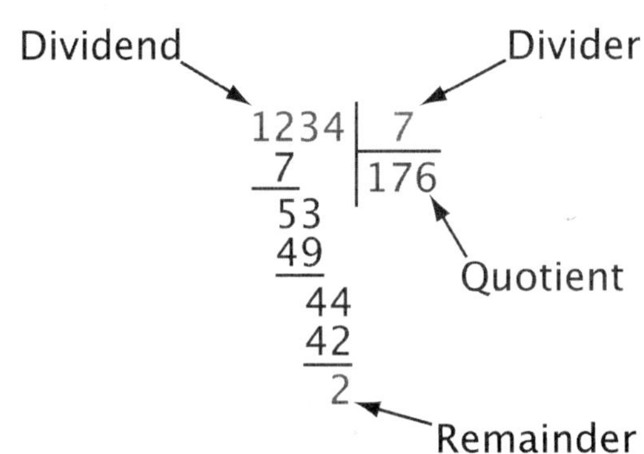


```
        1234 | 7
12-7=5   7↓  | 1
         53
```

```
          1234 | 7
           7   | 17
           53
53-49=4    49↓
            44
```

```
          1234 | 7
           7   | 176
           53
           49
            44
44-42=2     42
             2
```

5.2.5 The SMART Algorithm

The SMART algorithm is a step-by-step approach used to determine whether a number is divisible by another. Suppose you were given the number 988 and asked whether it was divisible by 7. The first step is always to subtract the divisor (in this case, 7) from 10. Here we get 3. Multiply the result (3) by the number farthest to the left (in this case, 9) to get a result of 27. Cross out the number farthest to the left (9) and add the result to the new number farthest to the left (in this case, the 8 in the tens place). The new number is 358. Repeat. $3 \times 3 = 9$ and add the 9 to the 5 in the tens place to get 148. Repeat. $1 \times 3 = 3$, cross out the 1 and add the 3 to the 4 now in the tens place to get 78. You could continue or you could recognize that, since 77 is a recognizable multiple of 7, the remainder is 1.

SMART → **S**igned **M**ultiplier **A**ddition **R**eduction **T**echnique.

Let's find the remainder of division of 988 by 7 using SMART.

(1) First, find the multiplier: 10 - 7 = 3. The multiplier is found by subtracting the divisor, in this case 7, from 10. For this method to work, the divisor must be between 1 and 19.

(2) The second step is to multiply the first digit of the original number, 9, by the *multiplier*, 3, and write it below the original number, as shown:

988
9x3=27
270
88+270=358
358

We write the product of the multiplication, 27, in such a way, that its last digit, 7, sits right under the second digit, 8, of the original number, 988.

(3) We now cancel the first digit of the original number and fill up the remaining digits to the right of 27 with zeros.

(4) Add the two resulting numbers to get: $88 + 270 = 358$.

(5) Repeat the steps until a single digit number is obtained, see below.

358
3x3=9
90
58+90=148
148

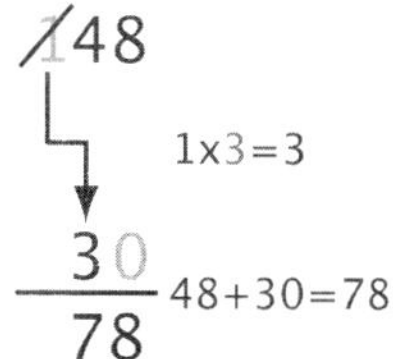

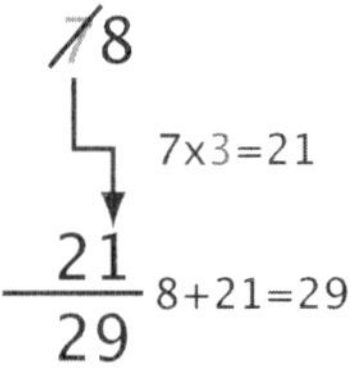

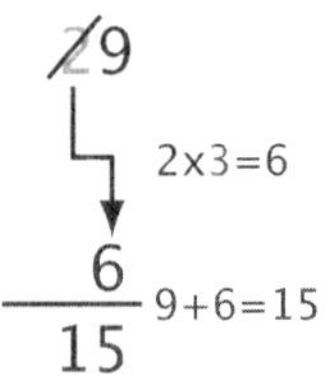

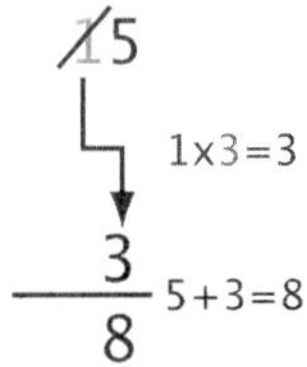

(6) In this example, the single digit number is 8. Then the remainder of division of 988 by 7 is: 8 - 7 = 1.

Again, the SMART algorithm is a two-step repetitive process that allows you to determine divisibility. After subtracting the divisor from 10,

(1) Multiply the result of that subtraction by the number farthest to the left.

(2) Cross that number out and add the result of the multiplication to the new number farthest to the left.

Repeat until you see a number you recognize as having a particular remainder.

This works for numbers larger than 10 as well. For example, suppose we wanted to see what the remainder was when 186 was the dividend and 13 the divisor. Subtracting 13 from 10, we get -3. $1 \times -3 = -3$, cancelling the 1 in the hundreds column and multiplying -3 by 1, then adding the result to the 8 in the tens column, we get 56. $5 \times -3 = -15$ and we subtract 15 from the 6 to get -9. Here we realize that we need to subtract 4 to get a number divisible by 13 (-13) and thus the remainder is 4.

Use SMART to find if 186 is divisible by 13.

186
1x(-3)=-3
-30
86+(-30)=56
56

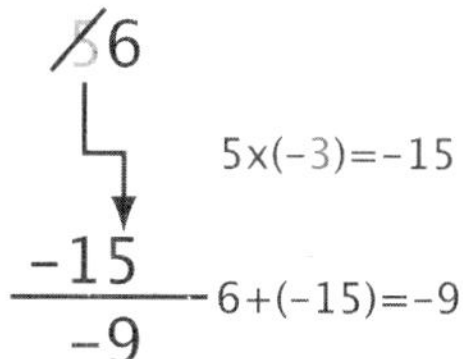

But suppose we wanted to test 838 for divisibility by 13. This throws in an additional wrinkle. Subtracting 13 from 10, we get -3. Multiply -3 by 8 to get -24. When the result of the addition will become negative, as it will in this case, the -24 becomes -240 and is added to the remaining 38 to get -202. Then flip the sign. Starting with 202, we multiply the leftmost 2 by -3 and add -60 to the remaining 02 to get -58. Flip the sign. 58 should be recognizable as having a remainder of 6 when divided by 13. Flipping the sign an even number of times will restore the remainder to the proper number.

But what happens when you are checking for divisibility by 13 of a number like 87? $8 \times -3 = -24$ and we get -17 when we add -24 to the remaining 7. Flip the sign. $1 \times (-3) = -3$ and we are left with 4 when we subtract 3 from 7. But we have only flipped the sign once. We need to do it again to restore the proper divisor. So it becomes -4. And if you add 13 to -4 you get 9, which is the remainder.

The general procedure when you get a negative result for the subtraction is:

After subtracting the divisor from 10,

(1) Multiply the result of the subtraction from the left-most digit.

(2) Add the (negative) result to the new left-most digit, filling in as many zeroes as needed to complete the number.

(3) Flip the sign to make the result positive.

Repeat. It is imperative that you flip the sign an even number of times to attain the proper result.

Use SMART to find if 613 is divisible by 13.

613

6x(-3)=-18

-180

13+(-180)=-167

-167

167

1x(-3)=-3

-30

67+(-30)=37

37

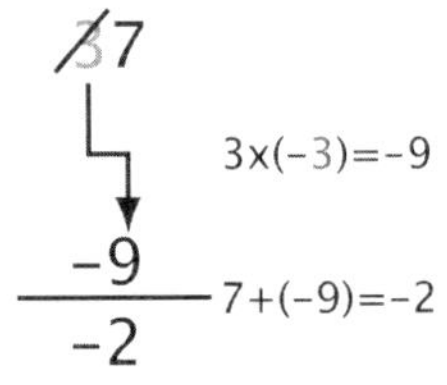

$$\begin{array}{r} \not{3}7 \\ \downarrow \quad 3\times(-3)=-9 \\ -9 \\ \hline -2 \end{array} \quad 7+(-9)=-2$$

Let's find the remainder of division of 1234 by 7 using SMART.

(1) Find the multiplier: 10 - 7 = 3.

(2) Multiply the first digit of the original number, 1, by the *multiplier*, 3, and write it below the original number, as shown:

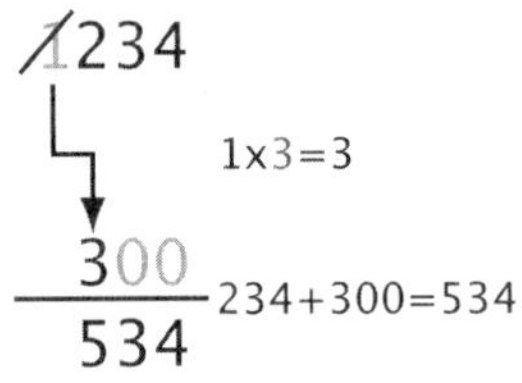

$$\begin{array}{r} \not{1}234 \\ \downarrow \quad 1\times3=3 \\ 300 \\ \hline 534 \end{array} \quad 234+300=534$$

(3) Cancel the first digit of the original number and fill up the remaining digits to the right of 3 with zeros.

(4) Add the two resulting numbers to get: 234 + 300 = 534.

(5) Repeat the steps until a single digit number is obtained.

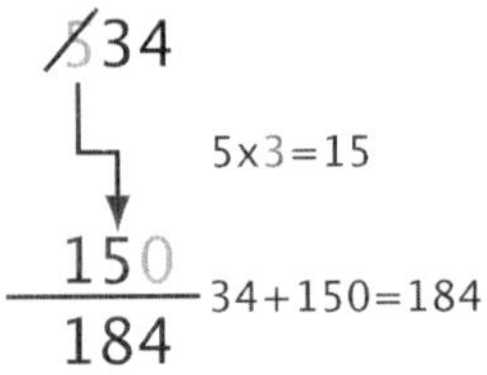

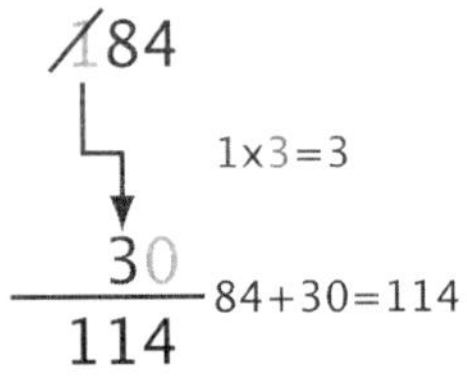

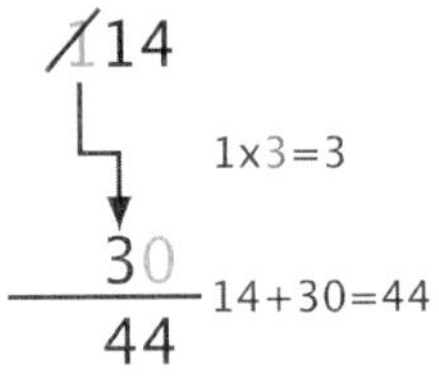

$$\begin{array}{r} \not{5}34 \\ \downarrow \quad 5\times3=15 \\ 150 \\ \hline 184 \end{array} \quad 34+150=184$$

$$\begin{array}{r} \not{1}84 \\ \downarrow \quad 1\times3=3 \\ 30 \\ \hline 114 \end{array} \quad 84+30=114$$

$$\begin{array}{r} \not{1}14 \\ \downarrow \quad 1\times3=3 \\ 30 \\ \hline 44 \end{array} \quad 14+30=44$$

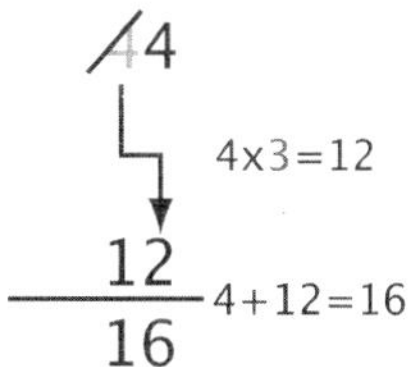

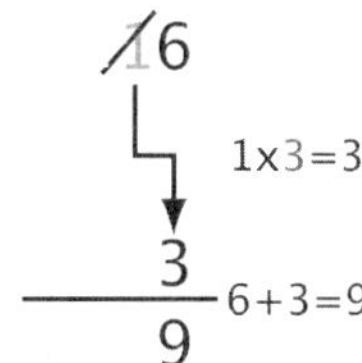

(6) The remainder of division is $9 - 7 = 2$.

Practice Problems

Use the SMART algorithm to:

(1) Find the remainder of 523 when divided by 7. Check with long division or chunking.

(2) Find the remainder of 813 when divided by 17. Check with long division or chunking.

5.2.6 Factorization Algorithm

If a given number is not prime, then the number must have at least one prime factor less than or equal to the square root of the original number.

This observation can now be used as the basis of the systematic search for factors of unfamiliar numbers. For example, is 133 prime? To find out, we will assume that it is not, and if our assumption is correct, one should be able to find at least one prime factor smaller than the square root of 133, which is between 11 and 12. Hence the only possible candidates are 2,3,5, 7 and 11. By inspection, both 2 and 5 are out, 11 is out because $11 \times 12 = 132$ and 3 is out because 133 does not satisfy the digit-sum test. But 7 satisfies the SMART check for 133, so 7 is a divisor and therefore, 133 is not prime.

Here are some other examples of prime factorization.

$$2100 = 2 \times 2 \times 3 \times 5 \times 5 \times 7$$

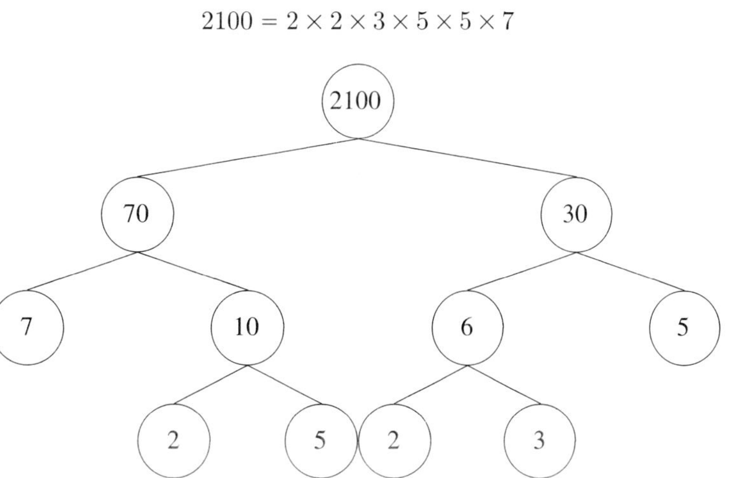

Divisible by:

35? 5×7 Yes

75? $3 \times 5 \times 5$ Yes

125? $5 \times 5 \times 5$ No

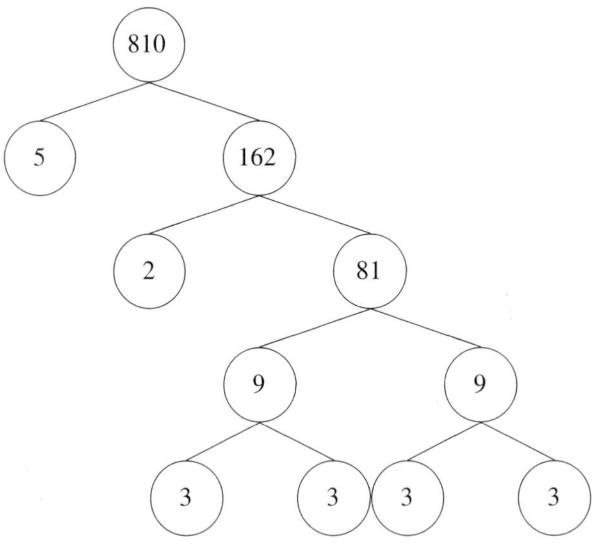

The Least Common Multiple (LCM) is the smallest multiple that is common to two or more numbers.

What is the LCM of 4, 7, 9 and 28?

$$4 = 2 \times 2$$
$$7 = 7 \times 1$$
$$9 = 3 \times 3$$
$$28 = 4 \times 7 = 2 \times 2 \times 7$$
$$\Rightarrow \text{LCM} = 2^2 \times 3^2 \times 7 = 4 \times 9 \times 7 = 252$$

The Greatest Common Factor (GCF) is the largest factor common to two or more numbers.

What is the GCF of 64 and 84?

$$64 = 2^2 \times 2^2 \times 2^2$$
$$84 = 2^2 \times 3 \times 7$$
$$\Rightarrow \text{GCF} = 2^2 = 4$$

$$9009 = 3 \times 3 \times 7 \times 11 \times 13$$

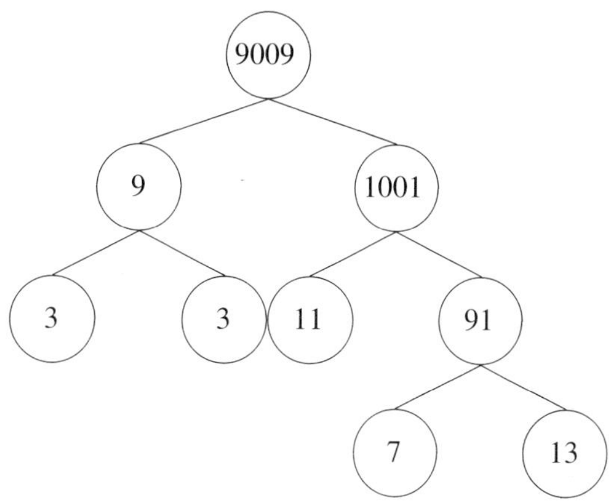

Student Notes:

5.3 Fractions

5.3.1 Types of Fractions

A *fraction* is a division of two numbers. The general form is $\frac{x}{y}$, where x is the **numerator** and y is the **denominator**. An important point to realize is that the denominator can never equal 0; it does not make sense mathematically to divide a number by 0.

Here are some examples of fractions $\frac{2}{7}, \frac{10}{9}, \frac{1}{3}, \frac{101}{72}, \frac{6}{8}$.

There are different types of fractions:

(1) **Simple Fraction**: It is the most common type of the fraction. A simple fraction, such as $\frac{5}{7}$, has both numerator and denominator as real numbers.

(2) **Complex Fraction**: A complex fraction differs from a simple fraction only by having either numerator, denominator or both as fractions. Thus, $\frac{4}{\frac{6}{8}}$, $\frac{\frac{1}{3}}{9}$ and $\frac{\frac{3}{11}}{\frac{10}{8}}$ are all complex fractions.

(3) **Proper Fraction**: As long as the numerator is less than the denominator (e.g. $\frac{5}{6}$), it is a proper fraction.

(4) **Improper Fraction**: On the other hand, if the denominator is less than the numerator (e.g. $\frac{10}{9}$), the fraction is improper.

(5) **Mixed Fraction**: A mixed fraction is a number and a proper fraction. For example $5 + \frac{2}{3}$ is a mixed fraction, and it is usually written as $5\frac{2}{3}$. When the denominator is less than the numerator, one can obtain a mixed fraction by dividing the numerator by the denominator. For example, $\frac{20}{7} = 2 + \frac{6}{7}$.

Student Notes:

5.3.2 Adding and Subtracting Fractions

If two fractions have the same denominator, they can be added or subtracted by simply performing corresponding operation with their numerators. For example:

$$\frac{3}{13} + \frac{5}{13} = \frac{3+5}{13} = \frac{8}{13} \text{(Note: Final value is increased.)}$$

$$\frac{12}{25} - \frac{4}{25} = \frac{12-4}{25} = \frac{8}{25} \text{(Note: Final value is decreased.)}$$

However, if two fractions have different denominators, first change them to equivalent fractions with the same denominator and only then add or subtract them. For example:

$$\frac{1}{8} + \frac{5}{9} = \frac{9}{72} + \frac{40}{72} = \frac{9+40}{72} = \frac{49}{72}$$

A common mistake would be to add both numerators and denominators separately (DO NOT DO THIS).

5.3.3 Equivalent Fractions

Usually a fraction should be **simplified** to lowest terms. One can do it by dividing both the numerator and the denominator by greatest common divisor. For example:

$$\frac{15}{45} = \frac{15 \times 1}{15 \times 3} = \frac{1}{3}$$

$$\frac{8}{20} = \frac{4 \times 2}{4 \times 5} = \frac{2}{5}$$

Often it is often also useful to convert a fraction in its simplest form into another form, particularly in ratio problems. For example, $\frac{2}{7}$ could be converted to:

$$\frac{2 \times 7}{7 \times 7} = \frac{14}{49}$$

If two fractions are equal after simplification, they are called **equivalent**. For example, $\frac{15}{24}$ and $\frac{10}{16}$ are equivalent as they both represent $\frac{5}{8}$:

$$\frac{15}{24} = \frac{15 \div 3}{24 \div 3} = \frac{5}{8}$$

$$\frac{10}{16} = \frac{10 \div 2}{16 \div 2} = \frac{5}{8}$$

Student Notes:

5.3.4 Multiplying and Dividing Fractions

Fraction multiplication and division are much simpler than addition and subtraction. To multiply two fractions, multiply their respective numerators and denominators. For example:

$$\frac{4}{17} \times \frac{3}{10} = \frac{12}{170} = \frac{6}{85} \text{(Note: Final value is decreased.)}$$

$$\frac{5}{3} \times \frac{12}{7} = \frac{5 \times 12}{3 \times 7} = \frac{60}{21} = \frac{20}{7}$$

To divide two fractions, **invert** the second fraction and complete multiplication. For example:

$$\frac{5}{8} \div \frac{3}{4} = \frac{5}{8} \times \frac{4}{3} = \frac{5}{6} \text{(Note: Final value is increased.)}$$

$$\frac{9}{14} \div \frac{3}{2} = \frac{9}{14} \times \frac{2}{3} = \frac{9 \times 2}{14 \times 3} = \frac{18}{42} = \frac{3}{7}$$

Practice Problems

(1) Change the following improper fractions into mixed fractions:

(a) $\frac{100}{9}$

(b) $\frac{13}{5}$

(c) $\frac{7}{2}$

(2) Change following mixed fractions into improper fractions:

(a) $3\frac{3}{7}$

(b) $4\frac{1}{11}$

(c) $1\frac{2}{5}$

(3) Simplify these fractions:

(a) $\frac{14}{26}$

(b) $\frac{100}{5}$

(c) $\frac{3}{6}$

(4) Perform the following calculations:

(a) $\frac{2}{9} + \frac{10}{11} + \frac{1}{3}$

(b) $\frac{14}{9} \times \frac{27}{4}$

(c) $\frac{75}{11} - \frac{7}{6}$

(d) $\frac{5}{77} \div \frac{25}{11}$

Student Notes:

5.3.5 Comparing Fractions

First, let us start with two fractions:

$$\frac{4}{7} \; ? \; \frac{5}{9}$$

$$\frac{4 \times 9}{7 \times 9} \; ? \; \frac{5 \times 7}{9 \times 7}$$

$$\frac{36}{63} \; ? \; \frac{35}{63}$$

$$\frac{36}{63} > \frac{35}{63}$$

If more than two fractions, compare pairwise:

$$\frac{2}{5}, \frac{3}{7}, \frac{5}{13}$$

$$\frac{2}{5} \; ? \; \frac{3}{7}$$

$$\frac{14}{35} \; ? \; \frac{15}{35}$$

$$\frac{14}{35} < \frac{15}{35}$$

$$\frac{3}{7} \; ? \; \frac{5}{13}$$

$$\frac{39}{91} \; ? \; \frac{35}{91}$$

$$\frac{39}{91} > \frac{35}{91}$$

$\frac{3}{7}$ is biggest fraction

5.4 Decimals

5.4.1 Introduction to Decimals

Besides the $\frac{numerator}{denominator}$ notation, fractions can also be written in **decimal** form. To obtain a decimal fraction from a usual fraction, just perform the division. For example, $\frac{1}{10} = 1 \div 10 = 0.1$. There are two types of decimals: **terminating** (for example, 0.63) and **infinite, repeating** (for example, 0.222...).

In decimal fractions, the position of **decimal point** (period) determines the place value of the digits. Thus, in 1234.5678, we have the following place values:

$$1234.5678$$

4 is in the 'ones' or 'units' place	5 is in the 'tenths' place
3 is in the 'tens' place	6 is in the 'hundredths' place
2 is in the 'hundreds' place	7 is in the 'thousandths' place
1 is in the 'thousands' place	8 is in the 'ten thousandths' place

5.4.2 Scientific Notation

It is also possible to write decimals as a product of a number with only one digit to the left of the decimal point and a power of 10, in **scientific notation.** For example,

$$5498 = 5.498 \times 10^3$$

$$0.00012 = 1.2 \times 10^{-4}$$

The scientific notation is usually used if we are interested in the magnitude of the number, and not all of its digits.

5.4.3 Changing Decimals to Fractions

5.4.3.1 Terminating Decimals

To change terminating decimals to regular fractions, remember the fact that all numbers to the right of a decimal point are fractions with the denominators of 10, 100, 1000, etc. For example,

$$0.003 = \frac{3}{1000}$$

$$0.1234 = \frac{1234}{10000}$$

$$0.2 = \frac{2}{10} = \frac{1}{5}$$

$$0.67 = \frac{67}{100}$$

If you can simplify the resulting fraction, you generally should, depending on how the answer is expressed. Not all answers are given in their simplest form.

Practice Problems

Perform the following calculations:

(1) Convert 0.239 into its simplest fractional form

(2) Convert $\frac{13}{40}$ into decimal form

(3) Convert 6.12×10^{-3} into its simplest fractional form

Student Notes:

5.4.3.2 Infinite Repeating Decimals

Suppose, we want to convert $0.23 = 0.2323$ First, suppose that 0.2323... equals x:

$$0.2323... = x$$

Then

$$23.2323... = 100x$$

Subtract first equation from second, and we get

$$23 = 99x$$

$$x = \frac{23}{99}$$

Thus, we found that $0.2323... = \frac{23}{99}$. In general, to convert an infinite repeating decimal to a fraction, find the least power of ten which gives you the same repeating **period** when you multiply original decimal by this power of ten. Then the decimal is equal to $\frac{period}{10^{power}-1}$.

Practice Problems

Identify each of the following as a terminating or infinite repeating decimal:

(1) $\frac{2}{11}$

(2) $\frac{1}{8}$

(3) $\frac{1}{9}$

Student Notes:

5.4.4 Operations with Decimals

5.4.4.1 Addition

To add two decimals, line up decimal points of both numbers. Often, one number will have fewer digits to the right of decimal point than the other. In such case, you can freely add zeroes to the right of the last digit as the number will not change. For example, to add 85.1234 and 4.981, write the numbers in a column:

$$\begin{array}{r} 85.1234 \\ \underline{+4.9810} \\ 90.1044 \end{array}$$

5.4.4.2 Subtraction

Subtraction works exactly like addition:

$$\begin{array}{r} 85.1234 \\ \underline{-4.9810} \\ 80.1424 \end{array}$$

5.4.4.3 Multiplication

To multiply two decimals, first multiply them as whole numbers. Then count the total number of digits to the right of the decimal point in the original two numbers. Thirdly, place the decimal point in the answer so that there is the same number of digits to the right of it.

For example, if we want to multiply 12.34 and 567.89, we first multiply 1234 and 56789: $1234 \times 56789 = 70077626$. There are two digits to the right of decimal in both 12.34 and 567.89, which makes it a total of four. Therefore, we count four digits from the right end of 70077626 and place decimal point there: 7007.7626.

$$12.34 \times 567.89 = 7007.7626$$

5.4.4.4 Division

Proceed with the division as usual if there is a decimal point only in the dividend. However, if there is a decimal point in the divisor, you should move it in both the divisor and the dividend until the divisor becomes a whole number. Then, just divide two numbers.

To prove the correctness of the method, assume we want to divide 65.98 by 2.1. The method suggests that it is the same as the division of 659.8 by 21. Indeed,

$$\frac{65.98}{2.1} = \frac{65.98 \times 10}{2.1 \times 10} = \frac{659.8}{21}$$

Often on the GMAT, you will see some complex-looking division problems involving decimals. Just move the decimal forward or backward to find an approximate solution. This technique will save you a lot of time.

$$1,830,895 \div (61.14 \times 10^4) \Rightarrow \frac{183 \times 10^4}{61.14 \times 10^4} \approx 3$$

Practice Problems

(1) Add the following decimal numbers:

(a) 3.2442, 4.004, -123.3

(b) -10.24, 345.544

(2) Multiply and divide the following decimal numbers:

(a) 234.434, 7.4

(b) 88.34, -4.53

Student Notes:

5.5 Real Numbers

5.5.1 Introduction

All **real** numbers correspond to points on the number line and vice versa. They can be either **positive**, **negative** or **zero** .

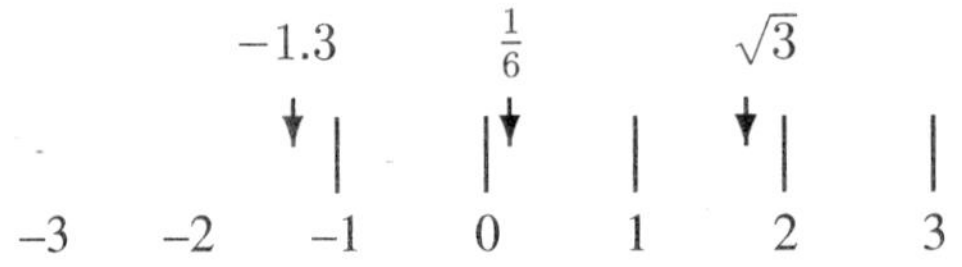

−1.3 $\frac{1}{6}$ $\sqrt{3}$

−3 −2 −1 0 1 2 3

Numbers corresponding to points on a number line to the left of zero are negatve and numbers corresponding to points to the right of zero are positive. For any two numbers, the number to the left is always less than the number to the right. Thus,

$$-20 < -5\frac{3}{4} < -\frac{8}{3} < 0 < 1.4 < 4$$

If y is between x and z on the number line, it means that $y > x$ and $y < z$, thus $x < y < z$. If y is 'between x and z, inclusive', then $x \leq y \leq z$.

5.6 Percentages and Interest

5.6.1 Percentage of and Percent Change

One of the most often tested concepts on the GMAT is percentages. It is very important for you to be able to distinguish between when the question asks you

(1) to express something as a percent of something else

(2) when the question asks you to find the percent change

In the first case, to say that x is n percent of y is to say, arithmetically,

$\frac{x}{y} = \frac{n}{100}$.

In the second case, the percent change formula can be expressed as follows:

$\%\text{ change} = \frac{F-I}{I} \times 100$

where F is the final value and I is the initial. An equivalent expression is:

$F = (1 + \frac{x\%}{100})I$

where x is the percent change. See if you can figure out why those two equations are equivalent.

Practice Problems

(1) What percent of 50 is 17?

(2) What is the percent change from 32 to 60?

(3) If a stock IPO'd at \$15 but over the course of the first day's trading jumped 150%, what would its closing price be?

Student Notes:

5.6.2 Interest

There are two different kinds of interest, simple and compound. For simple interest, the formula appears as follows:

$$R = P \times (1 + rt),$$

where R is the amount to be earned or returned, when P is the amount invested or borrowed, respectively. The interest rate r is measured on a per period basis. The period could be a year, a day, a minute, etc. The important thing is that the interest rate and the duration that the time is to be invested or borrowed have the same units. You can see that for simple interest, interest is only earned on the principal P.

For compound interest, the formula is a variation of the generic exponential growth expression:

$$R = P \times (1 + \frac{r}{n})^{nt},$$

where n indicates the number of compoundings per period and t must be expressed in terms of that particular time period. For example, for annual interest compounded quarterly, $n = 4$ and the time is expressed in years. If the interest were annual compounded monthly, $n = 12$. The more often the interest is compounded, the more interest is charged (earned).

Practice Problems

(1) If you borrowed \$500 at 10% simple annual interest for 3 years, how much would you have to repay?

(2) If you borrowed \$500 at 10% annual interest, compounded quarterly, for 3 years, how much would you have to repay? Just work out what the expression would look like.

Student Notes:

① $R = 500 \times (1 + 10\% \times 3)$

$= 500 \times 1.3$

$= 500 \times \frac{13}{10}$

6500

$= 650$

150 int

② $R = 500 \times (1 *$

$500 \times (1 + \frac{10\%}{4})^{3 \times 4}$

=

Student Notes:

Chapter 6

Algebra

6.1 Basic Concepts in Algebra

An algebraic expression is a relationship where letters and/or symbols represent numerical values. A number of differences arise, however, between algebraic and arithmetic relationships. In addition, mathematical shorthand is more common in algebraic relationships:

(1) The expression AB is taken to mean the value of A multiplied by the value of B. If $A = 5$ and $B = 7$, then AB equals 5×7.

(2) The expressions A^2 and B^3 is taken to mean $A \cdot A$ and $B \cdot B \cdot B$, respectively. Similarly, $5 \cdot 5$ or $(5)(5)$ is equivalent to 5 times 5 (or 25).

(3) There are rules to simplify the handling of expressions like A^2A^3. Since the first of these is $(A)(A)$ and the second is $(A)(A)(A)$, the result equals $(A)(A)(A)(A)(A)$. In shorter notation, this can be written as: $A^2A^3 = A^5$. This can be generalized to $A^rA^s = A^{r+s}$.

(4) The expression $A^{\frac{1}{2}}$ represents the square root of A. If $y = A^{\frac{1}{2}}$, then $Y^2 = A$. Similarly, $B^{\frac{1}{4}}$ is the fourth root of B.

(5) Mistakes that frequently occur when working on algebraic expressions include the following:

  (a) X^{-1} is not equal to $-X$. Nor are X^2 and Y^3 are the same as $2X$ and $3Y$.
  (b) $\frac{X+Y}{Z}$ is not equal to $\frac{X}{Z} + Y$. It does equal $\frac{X}{Z} + \frac{Y}{Z}$.
  (c) $(X + Y)^2$ is not the same as $X^2 + Y^2$, By FOIL, it equals $X^2 + 2XY + Y^2$.
  (d) $(X - Y)^2$ is not the same as $X^2 - Y^2$. By FOIL, it equals $X^2 - 2XY + Y^2$.
  (e) $5A + 3B$ is not equal to $15AB$.

(6) FOIL - Mnemonic for multiplying 2 binomials$(x + y)(x + y)$

  (a) F - First Terms: $x \cdot x$
  (b) O - Outside Terms: $x \cdot y$
  (c) I - Inside Terms: $y \cdot x$
  (d) L - Last Terms: $y \cdot y$

(7) A very useful algebraic relationship, often required in both arithmetic and geometrical problems as well, is:

$$X^2 - Y^2 = (X + Y)(X - Y)$$

6.2 Taking a SHOT at the Questions

Most of the math equations on the examinations can be made easier to handle if one or more of the following **S**uggestions, **H**ints, **O**bservations or **T**ricks are used:

(1) Attempt to illustrate the problem

Make a sketch of the problem; frequently, the very act of trying to diagram the question will suggest a method of solution:

For example: What is the value of $\frac{2}{3} + \frac{1}{6}$?

A graphical solution: Mark two lines of equal length, one above the other. Divide the top line into three equal segments and the bottom line into six equal segments. It becomes apparent that two of the top segments, i.e. $\frac{2}{3}$, plus one of the bottom segments equal the length of five of the bottom segments, i.e. $\frac{5}{6}$:

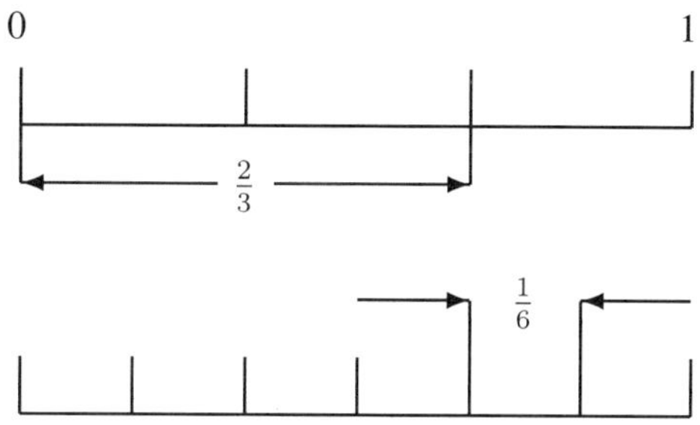

(2) Memorize common decimal/fraction equivalents

In descending order of importance, the following should be memorized:

$$\frac{1}{4} = 0.25, \quad \frac{1}{2} = 0.5, \quad \frac{3}{4} = 0.75, \quad \frac{1}{3} = 0.33\ldots, \quad \frac{2}{3} = 0.66\ldots$$

$$\frac{1}{8} = 0.125, \quad \frac{3}{8} = 0.375, \quad \frac{5}{8} = 0.625, \quad \frac{7}{8} = 0.875,$$

Less often needed is that $\frac{1}{9} = 0.111\ldots$. From this follows that $\frac{2}{9} = 0.222\ldots$, etc.

Student Notes:

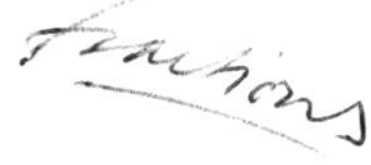

6.3 Do Not Multiply Out Intermediate Calculations

Exam questions are devised by examiners who usually prefer uncomplicated answers. To obtain this type of result generally means that complicated intermediate calculations must be simplified at the final stage. As an example:

If Y is $\frac{6}{7}$ of X, and Z is $\frac{2}{13}$ of Y, what is the value of Z when X takes on the value of 26?

(A) $\frac{321}{91}$ (B) $\frac{48}{13}$ (C) $\frac{156}{7}$ (D) $\frac{2,156}{137}$ (E) $\frac{24}{7}$

One might be expected to proceed as follows:

$Y = (\frac{6}{7})X$, since $X = 26$, then $Y = (\frac{6}{7})(26)$ or $Y = \frac{156}{7}$

[Note the temptation to pick C for an answer!] Continuing:

$$Z = (\frac{2}{13})(\frac{156}{7}) = \frac{312}{91}$$

and at this point choice A looks very close to the calculated result, but the correct answer is E. The trouble here is that, 13, is a factor of 156, but because the operation, 6 times 26, was carried out, the result 156 is not readily recognized as a multiple of 13. If the computation of Y had been left in its 'non-multiplied' format, then the calculation becomes:

$$Z = (\frac{2}{13})(\frac{6}{7})(26)$$

where it is apparent that the 13 will divide evenly into the 26.

Student Notes:

6.4 Avoid Working with Large Numbers

(Avoid operations that make large numbers into larger numbers.)

Most people become very cautious and slow down whenever they work with large numbers. Confronted with a large number, one often finds that routine numerical calculations become tiresome and disproportionally time-consuming. In these examinations, working slowly incurs one type of undeserved penalty on one's performance; on the other hand, attempting to work more rapidly brings its own penalties in the form of a marked increase in errors. It is clear that the use of simplifying procedures is always beneficial.

For example, if it were necessary to compute: $(26)^2 - (24)^2$

There is always a shortcut that does not require more than 1 minute to do the calculation. Therefore, anything that takes you longer will probably take you down the wrong path. One could certainly do the computation as stated, but this involves computing the squares of 26 and 24 and then calculating the difference between them. This time-consuming process is simplified by the use of the relationship given above:

$$X^2 - Y^2 = (X + Y)(X - Y)$$

Designating X as 26 and Y as 24 leads to $X + Y = 26 + 24 = 50$, and $X - Y = 26 - 24 = 2$, so $(X + Y)(X - Y) = (50)(2) = 100$, a conclusion reached in a fraction of the time needed to calculate the squares. The question could naturally arise, "... But how often is it necessary to calculate the difference between two squares?" Beyond arithmetic problems of the form shown above, one finds that this kind of computation is required frequently when using the Pythagorean Theorem for right triangles:

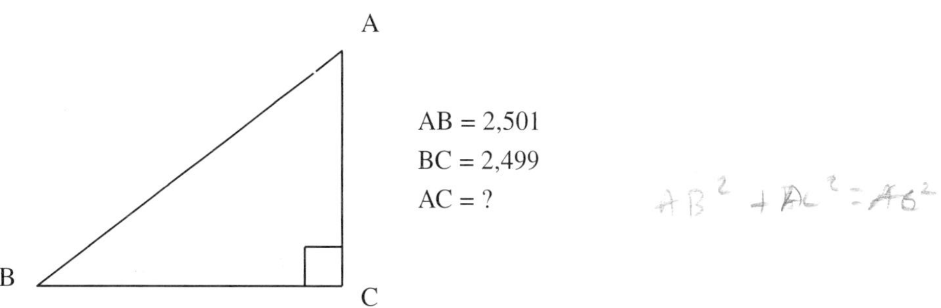

From the Pythagorean Theorem (See the chapter on Geometry):

$$\begin{aligned} (AC)^2 + (BC)^2 &= (AB)^2 \\ (AC)^2 &= (AB)^2 - (BC)^2 \\ &= (2,501)^2 - (2,499)^2 \end{aligned}$$

To solve this problem requires the calculation of the difference between two square, and this will proceed much faster using the above relationship because $2,501 + 2,499 = 5000$ and $2,501 - 2,499 = 2$ with the result that

$$(AC)^2 = (5,000)(2) = 10,000$$

Because this type of computation occurs so frequently, familiarity with this procedure is very useful.

Another example: What is the value of $5001^2 - 4999^2$?

$$(5001 + 4999)(5001 - 4999)$$

$$10000 \times 2 = 20000$$

Student Notes:

6.5 Algebra SHOTS

6.5.1 Manipulation of Equations

(a) Whenever feasible, simplify equations to permit processing with integer coefficients. In particular, avoid division operations whenever possible.

(b) Standard procedures for handling equations are to be found in any algebra text. However, the procedure below is not generally taught, although it can rapidly simplify intimidating relationships in appropriate cases. This procedure is based on the fact that for any given algebraic equation, the reciprocals of the complete relationship can be set equal. This means that any equation can be 'inverted' without loss of validity. As an example, consider:

$$\frac{1}{\frac{1}{X+2} - 3} = \frac{2}{3}$$

'Inverting' both sides of this equation gives:

$$\frac{1}{X+2} - 3 = \frac{3}{2}$$

Which gives:

$$\frac{1}{X+2} = \frac{9}{2}$$

Inverting once again produces:

$$\frac{X+2}{1} = \frac{2}{9}$$

From which:

$$X = -\frac{16}{9}$$

This procedure can be used (with care) in the processing of inequalities and this is described in the next section.

Practice Problems

Solve for x:

(1) $\frac{3}{\frac{2}{x-4}} = 1$

(2) $\frac{x+2}{\frac{x-6}{4}} = 3$

Student Notes:

6.5.2 Manipulation of Inequalities

The manipulation of inequalities follows exactly the same rules as those for equations with two exceptions. These are:

(a) The multiplication (or division) of an inequality by any negative number causes a reversal of direction of the inequality sign. It should be noted that changing the signs of all terms in a relationship is the mathematical equivalent of multiplying all terms by -1. Consequently, the expression

$$7 - 2X > -3 \qquad \text{becomes} \qquad -7 + 2X < 3$$

(b) The using of the 'inverting' technique suggested above for equations will also cause a reversal of direction of the inequality sign. For example,

$$\frac{7}{2} > \frac{3}{4} \qquad \text{becomes} \qquad 0 < \frac{2}{7} < \frac{4}{3}$$

What is the possible value(s) of X, if X is a positive integer that satisfies the relationship?

$$\frac{2}{7} > \frac{1}{2X-3} > \frac{2}{13}$$

$$\frac{7}{2} < \frac{2X-3}{1} < \frac{13}{2}$$

$$3\frac{1}{2} < 2X - 3 < 6\frac{1}{2}$$

$$6\frac{1}{2} < 2X < 9\frac{1}{2}$$

$$3\frac{1}{4} < X < 4\frac{3}{4}$$

$$X = 4$$

Another Example:

$$5 \geqq 4 - \frac{x}{3} \geqq 2$$

$$15 \geqq 12 - x \geqq 6$$

$$3 \geqq -x \geqq -6$$

$$-3 \leqq x \leqq 6$$

Student Notes:

6.6 Systems of Linear Equations

You may be called upon to solve for the point where two lines intersect in two dimensions, or at maximum, the point at which three planes intersect. Take some time to convince yourself that unless two lines are identical, they can intersect at most one point. It will be a little more difficult to visualize, but also try to convince yourself that three non-identical planes also intersect at one point. The intermediate step is to realize that any two of the planes will intersect in a line.

A question that has this form could look like the following: Suppose you were a bottled water manufacturer. Your factory rents for \$5000 per month. Each bottle of water costs \$0.25 to produce and your price to the distributor is \$0.75. How many bottles must you sell per month to break even? How many bottles must you sell to reach a profit of \$3000 per month?

The equation for the total cost per month is $C = 5000 + 0.25 \times B$ and the equation for the total revenue per month is $R = 0.75 \times B$. To break even, $R = C$. Solve for B, the number of bottles to be sold.

$5000 + 0.25B = 0.75B \rightarrow 5000 = 0.50B \rightarrow B = 10000.$

To make a profit of \$3000 per month, $0.75B - (5000 + 0.25B) = 3000 \rightarrow 0.50B = 8000 \rightarrow B = 16000.$

In general, there are two methods for solving linear equations.

Substitution

The first involves substitution. Remembering that the solution represents the point of intersection, this means that the x and the y values must be the same. Suppose we had two equations, $3x + 2y = 7$ and $2x + y = 9$. Making use of the second equation and rearranging it, $y = 9 - 2x$, we plug that into the first equation: $3x + 2(9 - 2x) = 7$. We simply made use of the fact that y **EQUALS** (is the same as) $9 - 2x$. Now we can solve for x, once we simplify. $3x + 18 - 4x = 7 \rightarrow x = 11$. Now that we know what x is, we can plug in its value into either equation to solve for y. $3(11) + 2y = 7 \rightarrow y = -13$. To ensure that your answer is correct, plug the values that you got for x and y into the equation that you did not use when you originally solved for y. $2(11) + (-13) = 9$.

Sample Problem Solving Question
(Source: GMAT Mini-Test. Reprinted with prior permission.)

If $x + 5y = 16$ and $x = -3y$, then $y =$

- ○ −24
- ○ −8
- ○ −2
- ○ 2
- ○ 8

EXPLANATION:
Substitution of the second equation into the first equation yields

$$\begin{aligned} (-3y) + 5y &= 16 \\ 2y &= 16 \\ y &= 8 \end{aligned}$$

Re-Formation

The second method involves manipulating the equations. Using the same two equations as before

$$\begin{aligned} 3x + 2y &= 7 \\ 2x + y &= 9 \end{aligned}$$

Using the fact that $2x + y = 9$, we also know that $-4x - 2y = -18$ because all we did was multiply the entire equation by (–2). Now we have

$$\begin{aligned} 3x + 2y &= 7 \\ -4x - 2y &= -18 \end{aligned}$$

} add and cancel

Now we can just add the two equations together, remembering to add only like terms, to get $-x = -11 \rightarrow x = 11$. Then we can plug in $x = 11$ to solve for y, as before.

There is the possibility, however unlikely, that you may be given a system of three linear equations to solve. For example,

$$\begin{aligned} 2x + y - 3z &= 3 \\ x - y + 2z &= 4 \\ 5x - 2y + z &= 4 \end{aligned}$$

The best way to proceed is to look for easy cancellations (in this case, the y. In this case, combining the first two equations will reduce the computation to (and the second step is to multiply the top equation by 2 and add it to the bottom equation)

$$\begin{aligned} 3x - z &= 7 \\ 9x - 5z &= 10 \end{aligned}$$

Multiply the top equation by (–3) then add to the bottom equation to get $-2z = -11$ or $z = \frac{11}{2}$. Now that you know what z is, substitute it back into the equations, leaving you with two equations and two unknowns, which you know how to do now.

What is the geometric interpretation of a linear equation with 2 variables? ⇒ Straight line

What are the possible outcomes, when you have two linear equations? ⇒ Intersect, parallel, same

How to find out?

$$\begin{cases} 3x + 5y = 4 \\ 9x + 15y = 13 \end{cases}$$

Make first coefficient identical:

$$\begin{cases} 9x + 15y = 12 \quad (\times 3) \\ 9x + 15y = 13 \end{cases}$$

→ Parallel

Practice Problems

(1) Solve:

$$\begin{aligned} 2x + 3y &= 3 \\ x - 2y &= 11 \end{aligned}$$

(2) Solve:

$$\begin{aligned} x + y + z &= 8 \\ 2x - 2y - z &= 4 \\ x + 3y + 2z &= 2 \end{aligned}$$

6.7 Quadratic Equations

You have three different methods of attack for quadratic equations and the one you choose should depend on your comfort level and the difficulty of the problem. The general form for the equation is: $ax^2 + bx + c = 0$.

(1) The Quadratic Formula: $x = \frac{-b \pm \sqrt{b^2-4ac}}{2a}$

(2) Factoring: this is almost always possible

(3) Plugging in: sometimes, the easiest thing to do is see which answer works

Some of the more difficult problems on the GMAT involve the quadratic equation. For example: A pizza place makes \$500 per night selling pizzas at its regular price. If the owner decided to lower the cost of each pizza by \$2, she would sell twenty more pizzas per night and make \$60 more. How many pizzas will she sell at the reduced price?

Set up the equation: P represents the number of pizzas and C the cost of each:

$$\begin{aligned} P \times C &= 500 \\ (P + 20) \times (C - 2) &= 560 \end{aligned}$$

If you see a scenario like this, the easiest thing to do, once you have set up the equations is to plug in the various answer choices. To solve this directly, you would have to:

- Express C in terms of P and plug that result into the other equation ($C = \frac{500}{P}$). $(P + 20) \times (\frac{500}{P} - 2) = 560$.
- See that multiplying the ENTIRE equation by P gives a quadratic. $(P + 20) \times (500 - 2P) = 560P$.
- Multiply it out and then solve by either factoring or using the quadratic formula: $2P^2 + 100P - 10000 = 0 \rightarrow (2P + 200)(P - 50) = 0$. Since the number of pizzas cannot be negative, $P = 50$. But remember what you are being asked for? The number of pizzas at the reduced price. $P + 20 = 70$.

Do you get the sense that this way would be time consuming and fraught with problem solving peril?

Factoring would give the answer as well. Prime factoring, $500 \to 5 \times 5 \times 5 \times 2 \times 2$. Trying the different arrangements can be done fairly quickly.

In general, when possible, factoring gives the results with less effort than the quadratic equation:

$3x^2 - 4x - 4 = 0$

The key lies in prime factorization: the coefficient of the $x2$ term can only be broken down into 3×1 and the constant term -4, can be either -2×2, -4×1. Which of these combinations will give the right coefficient for the x term? $(3x + 2)(x - 2)$.

Sample Problem Solving Question
(Source: GMAT Mini-Test. Reprinted with prior permission.)

Which of the following equations has a root in common with $x^2 - 6x + 5 = 0$?

- ○ $x^2 + 1 = 0$
- ○ $x^2 - x - 2 = 0$
- ○ $x^2 - 10x - 5 = 0$
- ○ $2x^2 - 2 = 0$
- ○ $x^2 - 2x - 3 = 0$

EXPLANATION:

Since $x^2 - 6x + 5 = (x - 5)(x - 1)$, the roots of $x^2 - 6x + 5 = 0$ are 1 and 5. When these two values are substituted in each of the five choices to determine whether or not they satisfy the equation, only in the fourth choice does a value satisfy the equation, namely, $2(1)^2 - 2 = 0$. Thus the best answer is $2x^2 - 2 = 0$.

More Examples:

$$x^2 - 3x + 2$$
$$+1, +2 \text{ or } -1, -2?$$
$$(x - 1)(x - 2)$$

$\Rightarrow$ Roots $x_1 = 1$ and $x_2 = 2$

$$x^2 + 2x - 35$$
$$-1, +35 \text{ or } +1, -35 \text{ or}$$
$$-5, +7 \text{ or } +5, -7 \text{ or ?}$$
$$(x - 5)(x + 7)$$

$\Rightarrow$ Roots $x_1 = 5$ and $x_2 = -7$

Practice Problems

(1) Solve using the quadratic equation and by factoring: $2x^2 + 3x + 1 = 0$. Are the answers for each method the same? If not, check again.

(2) If 3 is one solution of the equation $x^2 - 5x + b = 10$, where b is a constant, what is the other solution?

6.8 Exponents & Roots

6.8.1 Exponents

The expression 9^2 is called a "*power*". In this case, it is a "*power of 9*". The number 9 is called the "*base*". The number 2 is called the "*exponent*"

Always remember: Exponents are just repeated multiplication. So increasing exponents means 'multiply this more times'.

To multiply powers with the same base, keep the base and add the exponents.

Examples:

$$2^3 \times 2^7 = 2^{10}$$

$$7^{19} \times 7^{13} = 7^{32}$$

To divide powers with the same base, keep the base and subtract the exponents.

Examples:

$$3^{25}/3^6 = 3^{19}$$

$$2^6/2^4 = 2^2$$

To raise a power to a power, multiply the exponents.

Examples:

$$(5^{10})^2 = 5^{20}$$

$$(3^4)^7 = 3^{28}$$

To multiply powers with the same exponent, keep the exponent and multiply the bases.

Examples:

$$3^9 \times 5^9 = 15^9$$

$$7^3 \times 5^3 = 35^3$$

6.8.2 Roots

A square root is the number which, multiplied by itself, gives the number under the radical sign.

A cube root is the number which, multiplied by itself twice, gives the number under the radical sign.

The square root sign in the GMAT means the *positive* square root.

Important to know the Perfect Square:

1 4 9 16 25 36 49 64 81 100 121 144 169 196 225

400 625 900 1600 2500

The examples of application of square roots can be seen in Geometry problems where the calculation of the hypotenuse is required.

Examples of estimated value of the square root of a non-perfect square:

$$\sqrt{2} \approx 1.414$$
$$\sqrt{3} \approx 1.732$$

Rules of Square Roots
Product of Square Roots = Square Root of the Product

Example:

$$\sqrt{3} \times \sqrt{5} = \sqrt{15}$$

Quotient of Square Roots = Square Root of the Quotient

Example:

$$\frac{\sqrt{15}}{\sqrt{5}} = \sqrt{\frac{15}{5}} = \sqrt{3}$$

Power of Square Roots = Square Root of the Power

Example:

$$(\sqrt{3})^3 = \sqrt{3^3} = \sqrt{27}$$

Adding Square Roots: You can NOT simplify the sum of square roots if they have different values inside the radical.

Example:

$\sqrt{3} + \sqrt{5}$ is already in its simplified form.

But if the numbers inside the radical are the same, then you can add the number in front of the radical (coefficient).

Example:

$$4\sqrt{5} + 3\sqrt{5} = 7\sqrt{5}$$

Simplifying Square Roots

First factor out the perfect squares inside the radical, then put the un-squared result in front of the radical.

Examples:

$$\sqrt{500} = \sqrt{5 \times 10^2} = 10\sqrt{5}$$
$$4\sqrt{500} = 4\sqrt{5 \times 10^2} = 40\sqrt{5}$$

To simplify an expression that has a square root in the denominator, just multiply both the numerator and denuminator by the same square root. This process is known as "*rationalizing the denominator*".

Examples:

$$\frac{3\sqrt{7}}{7\sqrt{3}} = \frac{3\sqrt{7}\times\sqrt{3}}{7\sqrt{3}\times\sqrt{3}} = \frac{3\sqrt{21}}{7\times 3} = \frac{\sqrt{21}}{7}$$
$$\frac{\sqrt{5}}{\sqrt{2}} = \frac{\sqrt{5}\times\sqrt{2}}{\sqrt{2}\times\sqrt{2}} = \frac{\sqrt{10}}{2}$$
$$\text{or } \frac{\sqrt{5}}{\sqrt{2}} = \sqrt{\frac{5}{2}} = \sqrt{\frac{5\times 2}{2\times 2}} = \frac{\sqrt{10}}{2}$$
$$\text{or } \frac{\sqrt{10}}{2} = \frac{\sqrt{5}\times\sqrt{2}}{\sqrt{2}\times\sqrt{2}} = \frac{\sqrt{5}}{\sqrt{2}}$$

6.8.3 Formulae Review

(1) $x^a \cdot x^b = x^{a+b}$

(2) $\frac{x^a}{x^b} = x^{a-b}$

(3) $x^a \cdot y^a = (xy)^a$

(4) $\left(\frac{x}{y}\right)^a = \frac{x^a}{y^a}$

(5) $(x^a)^b = x^{ab}$

(6) $x^{-a} = \frac{1}{x^a}$

(7) $x^0 = 1$, unless $x = 0$.

(8) $x^{\frac{a}{b}} = \sqrt[b]{x^a}$

(9) $\sqrt[n]{x} = x^{\frac{1}{n}}$

Practice Problems

(1) What is $2^3 \times 2^5$?

(2) What is $2^5 \div 2^3$?

(3) What is $(2^3)^2$?

(4) What is $16^{\frac{3}{4}}$?

Student Notes:

Chapter 7

Geometry

7.1 Basic Concepts in Geometry

While the percentage of geometry questions out of the entire question pool is falling, you are more likely to see a higher percentage of them when you are testing in the upper percentiles.

Almost any commercially available examination guide (including the 'Official Guide for GMAT Review') will provide an extensive summary of the geometrical relationships that may be required on the examination. The following is a checklist of what you will be expected to know:

(1) Terminology and properties

   (a) Angles: right angle, straight angle, acute/obtuse angles and triangles, supplementary and complementary angles
   (b) Right, isosceles and/or equilateral triangles
   (c) Parallelogram, rhombus, rectangle, square, trapezoid, trapezium

(2) Measurement of angles in

   (a) a triangle
   (b) polygons, particularly quadrilaterals
   (c) parallel lines crossed by an intersecting line
   (d) circles

(3) Measurement of lengths, areas and volumes in

   (a) quadrilaterals
   (b) triangles
   (c) circles
   (d) solids, such as prisms, pyramids, cylinders, spheres

Student Notes:

7.2 Properties of Angles

Given two intersecting lines or line segments, the amount of rotation about the point of intersection (the vertex) required to bring one into correspondence with the other is the angle between them.

Acute	$x < 90$
Right	$x = 90$
Obtuse	$90 < x < 180$
Straight	$x = 180$

perpendicular: lines that intersect with a 90° angle complementary: x + y = 90
supplementary: x + y = 180

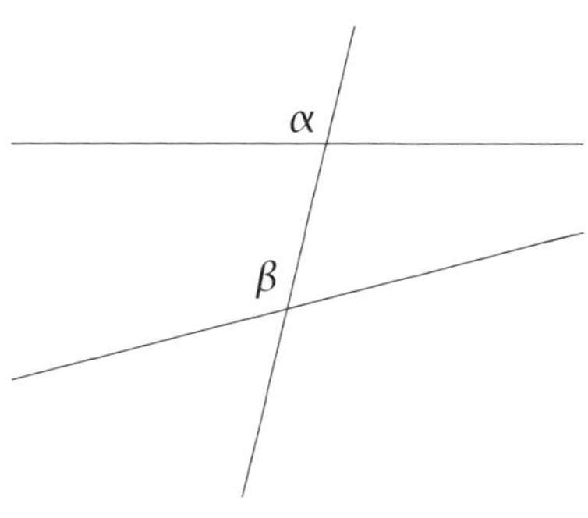

$\alpha = \beta$ **only** if $l_1 \| l_2$

Geometry problems differ fundamentally from algebra problems. In algebra, it is a largely process-driven approach to solving the problem. In geometry, the process is much more informationally driven. Much of the information in geometry problems will not be given, instead, will have to be inferred. To take a simple example, the figure below shows a line intersecting two other parallel lines, forming vertical angles, alternate interior angles and alternate exterior angles.

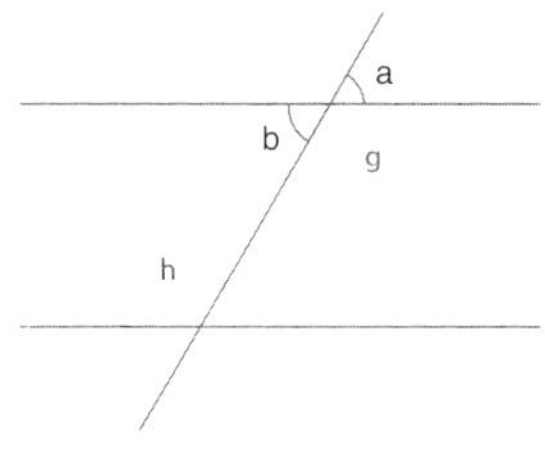

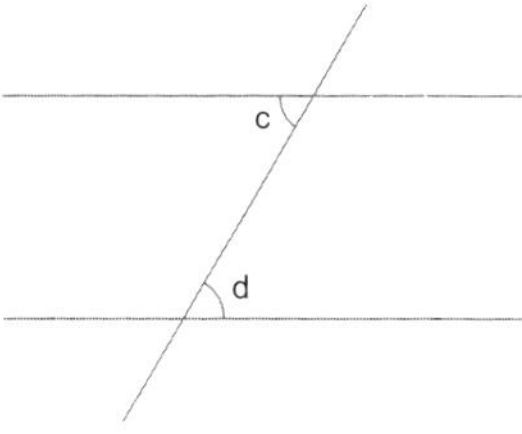

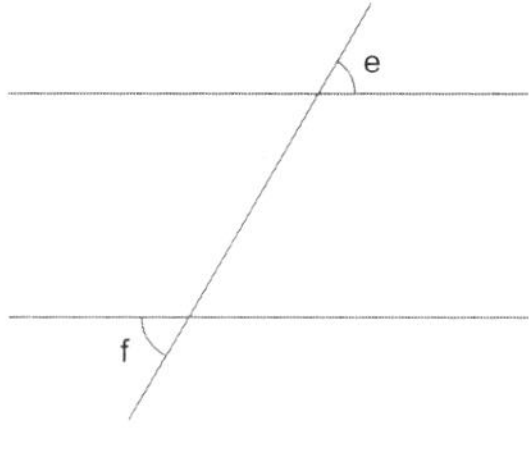

$a = b, g = h$
$a + g = 180°$
$b + h = 180°$

$c = d$

$e = f$

Any time two straight lines intersect, the opposite angles are equal and the adjacent angles must add to $180°$. This is never stated but can and must be used. Furthermore, when a line cuts through parallel lines, the angles that share the same relationship with the intersecting line must be equal. Thus, from one piece of information, we are able to glean several more. The ability to identify this kind of information is critical, particularly on the Data Sufficiency questions.

7.3 Triangles

A triangle is a shape formed by connecting the points of intersection of three mutually non-parallel lines. There are three kinds of triangles: acute (the largest angle has a measure less than $90°$, obtuse (the largest angle has a measure greater than $90°$, and right (the largest angle measures exactly $90°$). Two important things to note are

- The sum of the measures of the three angles of a triangle must be $180°$
- The sum of the lengths of two sides of the triangle must always exceed the third (the shortest distance between two points is a straight line)

>90

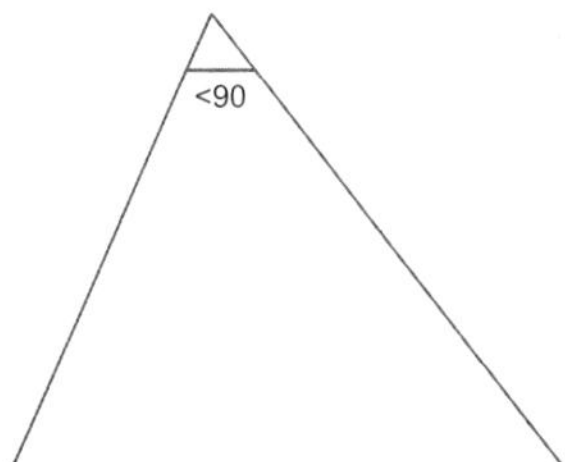

a b c

$$a + b > c$$
$$a + c > b$$
$$b + c > a$$

The perimeter P of a triangle is given by the sum of the lengths of the sides and the area A is given by $A = \frac{1}{2}bh$, where b is the base (which you are free to choose, according to the composition of the problem) and h is the perpendicular distance from the base to the opposing vertex .

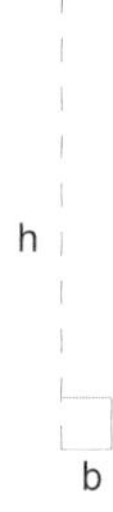

Isosceles triangles are triangles with at least two sides of equal length, and hence at least two angles of equal measure. One of their special properties, therefore, is that when a perpendicular is dropped from the vertex of the equal length sides to the third side, two right triangles are formed.

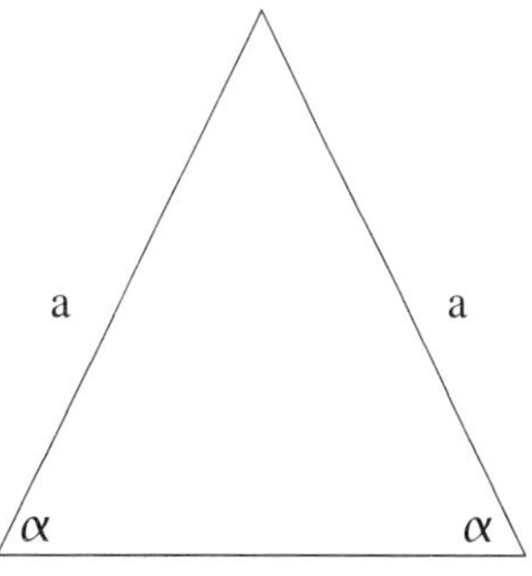

ISOSCELES

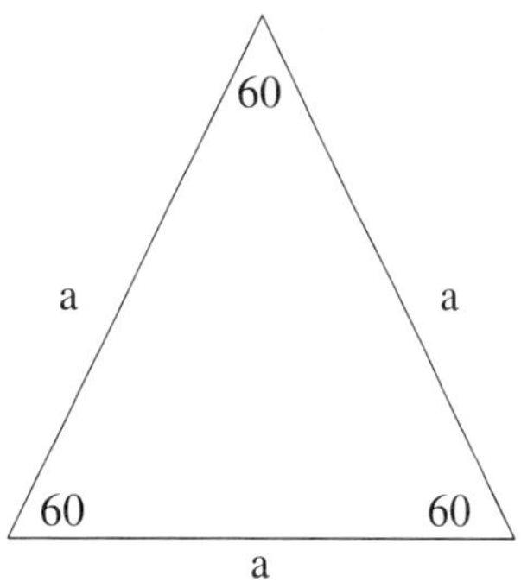

EQUILATERAL

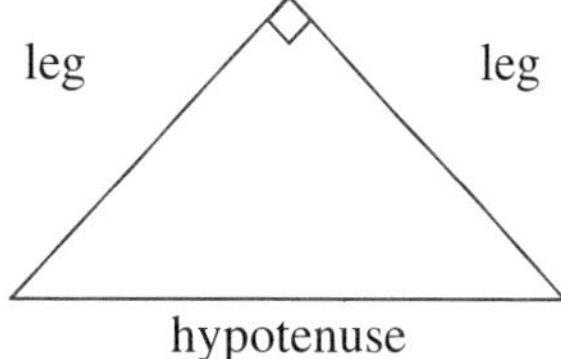

7.3.1 Right Triangle Relationships

The overwhelming majority of problems involving right triangles are based on just four configurations. These are:

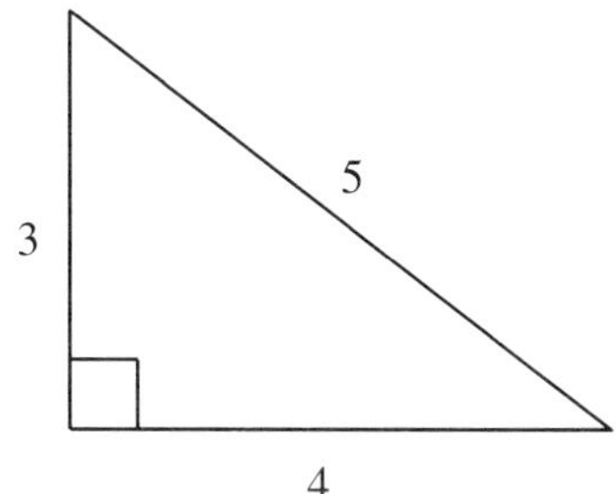

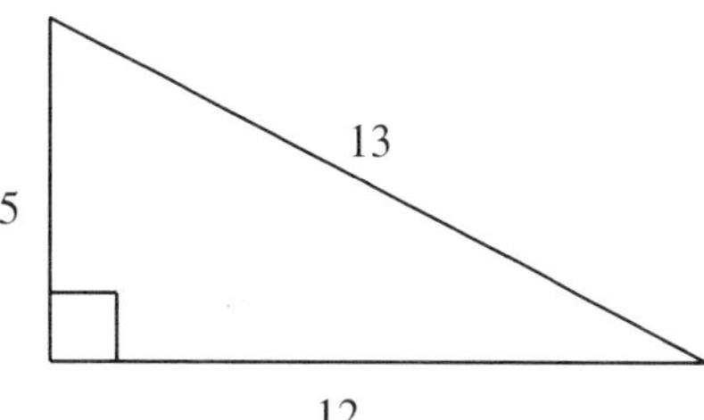

Two configurations with integer values for the lengths of the sides. (No questions will be posed regarding the angles of these two triangles.)

Two configurations involving particular sets of angles, these are the $45^\circ - 45^\circ - 90^\circ$ and the $30^\circ - 60^\circ - 90^\circ$ right triangles. The relative lengths of the sides of these triangles are determined by the size of the angles.

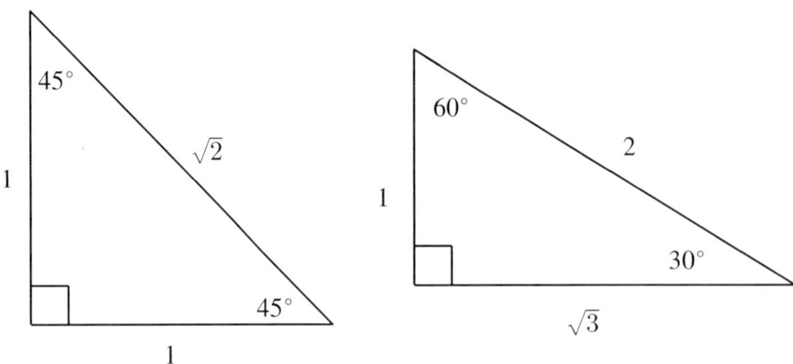

Practice Problems

(1) What is the area of an equilateral triangle with side 4?

(2) If a triangle has two sides of length 5 and 8, what is the range of values that the length of the third side take?

7.3.2 The Pythagorean Theorem

The Pythagorean Theorem is such an important concept on the GMAT, that although the theorem focuses strictly on triangles (and specifically right triangles), we have devoted an entire section to it.

The Pythagorean Theorem: For a right triangle, when the sides of the triangle are given by a, b, and c is the hypotenuse (the side opposite the right angle), the following relationship always holds:

$$a^2 + b^2 = c^2$$

If you need convincing, do the following: Get a sheet of graph paper and cut out squares such that the sum of the areas of the smaller two equals the area of the largest. When you arrange the vertices of the squares such that one of the vertices of each square touches one of the other two squares, you will have created a right triangle. Guaranteed.

Some of the more difficult geometry problems involve multiple applications of the Pythagorean theorem. An example of such a problem would be finding the greatest distance between two points on a rectangular box. Whenever necessary, draw a picture, if one is not given, particularly for geometry problems. Supposing that the length of the box were given by l, the width by w, and the height by h, the diagonal across the rectangle of length l and width w would have length $\sqrt{l^2 + w^2}$. The diagonal formed across the length and the width of the rectangle is still perpendicular to the height. The triangle formed by the two is still subject to the Pythagorean Theorem and the hypotenuse of the new triangle is $\sqrt{l^2 + w^2 + h^2}$.

Typical right triangle relationships are

$$3 - 4 - 5$$
$$5 - 12 - 13$$
$$7 - 24 - 25$$

and

$$8 - 15 - 17$$

Multiples of these ratios are also right triangle relationships, for example,

$$6 - 8 - 10$$
$$10 - 24 - 26$$

Practice Problems

(1) What is the hypotenuse of a right triangle with sides of length $\sqrt{17}$ and 8?

(2) Which of the following does not describe the relationship of sides of a right triangle?

1. 15-20-25 2. 9-40-41 3. 8-12-16

7.3.3 Scalene Triangles

Scalene triangles are triangles with no equal angles or sides. They will almost never appear on the GMAT and are shown here for your future reference. A not widely known, but potentially very useful formula for determining the area of any triangle with sides of length a, b, and c is Hero's Formula, given by:

$A = \sqrt{s(s-a)(s-b)(s-c)}$

where $s = \frac{a+b+c}{2}$.

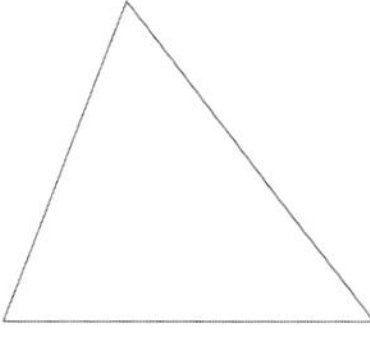

Practice Problem

What is the area of a triangle with sides 8, 12, 16?

7.3.4 Formulae Review

Triangles

(1) Sum of the angles: $\angle A + \angle B + \angle C = 180°$

(2) Area of a triangle: $A = \frac{1}{2}bh$ or
Hero's Formula: $A = \sqrt{s(s-a)(s-b)(s-c)}$, where $s = \frac{a+b+c}{2}$

(3) Relationships among sides of a triangle: $a + b > c$, $a + c > b$, and $b + c > a$

(4) Perimeter of a triangle: $P = a + b + c$

(5) Right triangles: Pythagorean Theorem $a^2 + b^2 = c^2$

7.4 The Equation of a Line

The infamous formula $y = mx + b$ represents the equation of a line with slope m and y-intercept b. The y-intercept is the point at which the line crosses the y-axis, meaning that the x-coordinate of y-intercept is zero. So we have one point of the line $y = b, x = 0$, represented by (0,b).

The x-intercept (where the line crosses the x-axis, in other words, when $y = 0$) can also be found: $0 = mx + b \rightarrow x = -b/m$.

Once you have found the x- and the y-intercepts, you can plot the two points, connect the dots, and that represents the line.

The slope m is the rise over the run in your old high school vernacular, where the run is the number of x-units and the rise is the number of y-units to be traveled to reach the next point. The larger the slope, the steeper the line. A slope of 0 gives a horizontal line (only x changes, y is constant). A slope of 1 gives a line that makes a 45° angle with the x-axis.

If you know two points on the line, you can find the slope m:

$$m = \frac{y_2 - y_1}{x_2 - x_1},$$

where the subscript 1 represents the first point and the subscript 2 the second, which is the same idea as the rise over the run. Once you find the slope, you can use one of the two points given to find the y-intercept, because you know x, y, and m; the only thing left is b and you have the equation to solve for it.

Practice Problems

(1) What is the equation of the line that intersects (2,3) and (5,8)?

(2) What is the x-intercept of the line $y = 3x - 5$?

(3) If $y = -\frac{1}{2}x + 3$, what is x when $y = 6$?

7.4.1 Coordinate Geometry

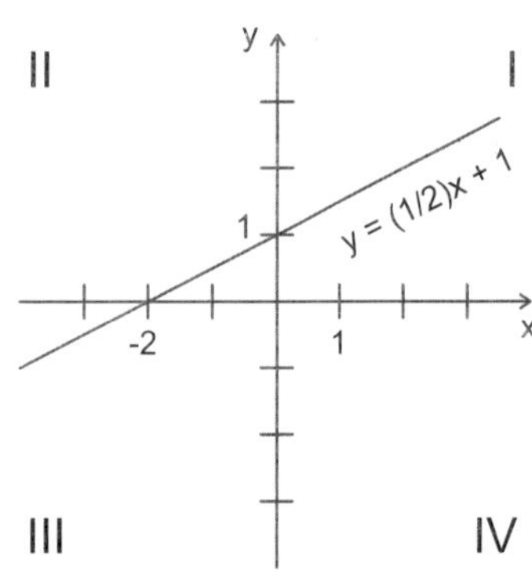

Quadrant	Value of X	Value of Y
I	+	+
II	-	+
III	-	-
IV	+	-

Properties of a line: $y = mx + b$

(1) Slope: $m = \frac{y_2 - y_1}{x_2 - x_1}$

(2) X-intercept = $-b/m$

Slope Type	Orientation
Positive	/
Negative	\
Zero	Horizontal
Undefined	Vertical

Intercept	Coordinates
x	$(x, 0)$
y	$(0, y)$

Coordinate geometry, as far as the GMAT is concerned, has largely to do with finding distances between points and being able to grasp the relationship between the equation of a line and its graphic representation. In the above line, the equation given by $y = \frac{1}{2}x + 1$, we can see that the graphic representation matches the equation. Pick any x and the y value you obtain will match the coordinates of that particular point on the line.

To find the distance between two points, use the Pythagorean Theorem (is there no end to its usefulness?). Given two points (x_1, y_1) and (x_2, y_2), you can see that a right triangle is made by drawing one line parallel to the x-axis that goes through one of the points and a line parallel to the y-axis such that these two lines intersect each other. The lengths of the two sides are: $|y_1 - y_2|$ and $|x_1 - x_2|$. The hypotenuse is therefore $\sqrt{(y_1 - y_2)^2 + (x_1 - x_2)^2}$, and you have found the distance between the two points.

Another popular problem is finding areas of triangles made by intersecting lines. Almost invariably, the triangle will be a right triangle. Just remember that the $A = \frac{1}{2}bh$ and use the two legs of the triangle to find the base and the height. The problem should proceed smoothly thereafter.

Practice Problems

(1) What is the area of the region bounded by the x-axis, the y-axis, and the line $y = 6 - 3x$?

(2) What is the area of the line bounded by the y-axis, $y = x$, and $y = 4$?

(3) What is the distance between the points $(2, 3)$ and $(-3, -9)$?

7.5 Quadrilaterals

Starting from greatest symmetry to least,

Type of Quadrilateral	Perimeter	Area	Features
Square	$4l$	l^2	All sides equal & parallel, all angles 90°, diagonal=$\sqrt{2}l$.
Rectangle	$2l + 2w$	lw	Opposite sides equal & parallel, all angles 90°
Parallelogram	$2a + 2b$	bh	Opposite sides equal & parallel, opposite angles equal
Rhombus	$2a + 2b$	$\frac{1}{2}(d \times d)$ (d - diagonal)	All sides equal, opposite angles equal, perpendicular diagonals
Trapezoid	$a + b + c + d$	$\frac{1}{2}(a + c)h$	One pair of sides parallel (sides a and c)
Trapezium	$a + b + c + d$	Not easily determined	No sides parallel

Fortunately, trapezia are so difficult to work with that they very seldom appear in GMAT questions.

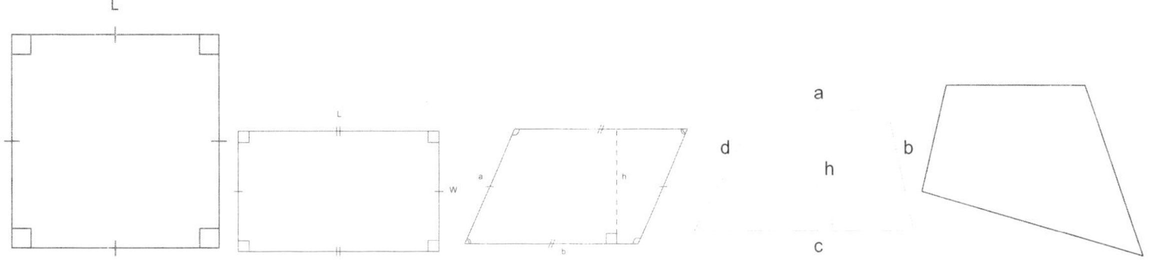

Practice Problems

(1) What is the area of a square with perimeter 8?

(2) A rectangle with a length three times its width has a perimeter of 16. What is its area?

(3) A parallelogram with an interior angle of 45° has a height of 5 and a base of 10. What is its perimeter?

(4) A trapezoid with height 6 has an area of 42. What is the average length of the parallel sides?

7.6 Other Polygons

Questions involving polygons with more than four sides rarely appear. Should one appear, however, it is very likely that it will be regular (*i.e.* have all sides equal in length). In this case, important formulae to know are that the total of all the interior angles of a regular polygon is given by $(n-2)\times 180°$ and a single angle is $\frac{n-2}{n}\times 180°$, where n is the number of sides of the polygon. You can see this by drawing lines from one vertex to the rest. There will be $n-2$ triangles and n interior angles. A regular hexagon is particularly interesting because the interior angles are $120°$ and when bisected form $60°$ angles. Regular hexagons can thus be subdivided into six equilateral triangles, the ramifications of which should be apparent.

Examples of polygons with more than four sides include pentagon, hexagon (2 below), heptagon, octagon, nonagon and decagon.

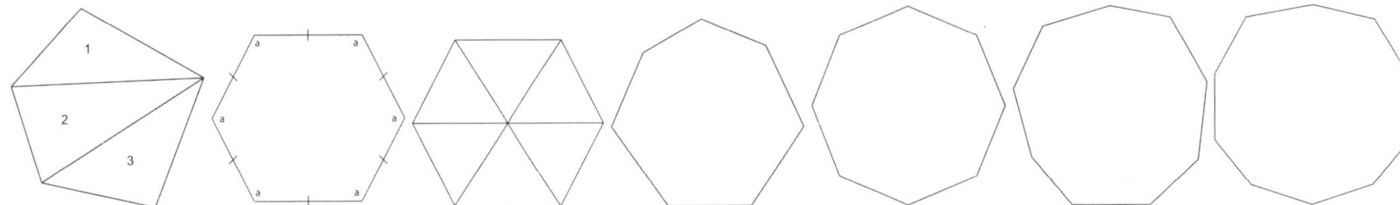

7.6.1 Terminology of Polygons

A diagonal of a polygon is a line segment that connects one vertex with another vertex and is not itself a side.

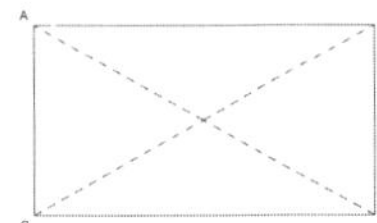

A convex polygon has all diagonals within the figure, meaning that if you choose two vertices and draw a line between them, the line will be entirely within the figure.

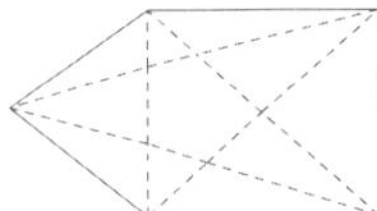

A concave polygon has at least one diagonal that extends outside the figure.

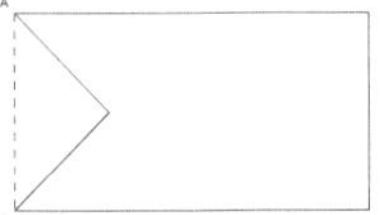

7.7 Circles

A circle is the set of points in a two-dimensional plane equidistant from a particular point, called the center. The area of a circle is πr^2, r being the distance from the center to each of these points and π an irrational number approximately equal to 3.14. The circumference of the circle (the equivalent of the perimeter) is $2\pi r$.

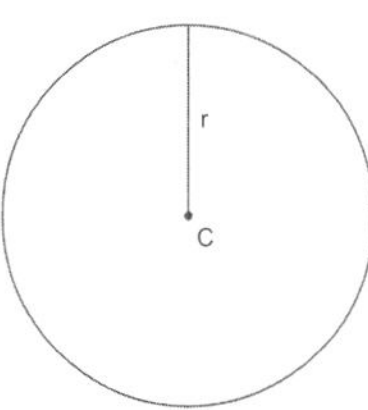

An important relationship to know is the one that compares the length of an arc (a part of the circle) with the angle that the sector (a pie-shaped slice of the circle with the vertex at the center of the circle)

$$\frac{l}{2\pi r} = \frac{\alpha}{360^\circ}$$

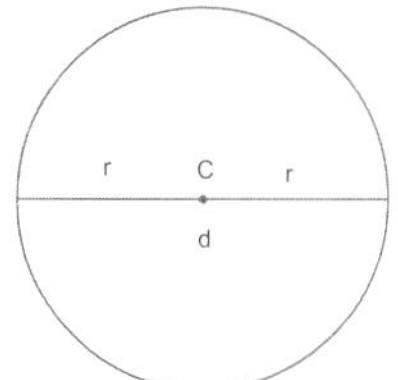

Another extremely important point to know is that if a central angle (an angle made by two radii) subtends a particular arc and has an angle α, the angle made by picking a third point on the circle, rather than from the center will be exactly $\alpha/2$. This has important implications relating to inscribed triangles, as we shall see shortly. To clarify, drawing a diameter across the circle makes an angle of 180°. Starting at one end of the diameter, drawing a straight line to *any* other point on the circle, then going to the other end of the diameter will give an angle of 90°.

$$\text{Inscribed Angle} = \frac{1}{2} \times \text{Central Angle}$$

One more: a line tangent to a circle is perpendicular to the radius of that circle drawn from the point of tangency.

Other terms relating to circles include the diameter (twice the radius, also the greatest distance between two points on a circle), a chord, which is the line segment connecting any two points on a circle, and a tangent, which is the line touching, but not intersecting a circle.

7.8 Polygons Inscribed In Circles

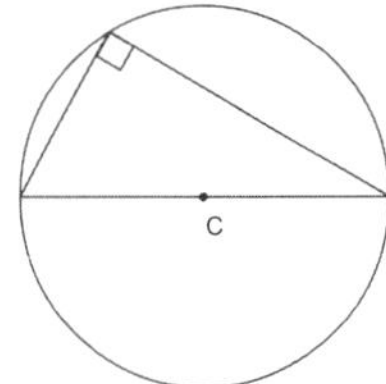

If a triangle is inscribed inside a circle and the diameter makes up two of the points of the triangle, the triangle is a right triangle. It is called the Triangle of Thales. This is one of those little known facts that you can use to impress your friends at parties. Clearly, there is a wealth of problems that can be generated by inscribing right triangles in circles. The recommendation, therefore, is to make yourself very familiar with this arrangement.

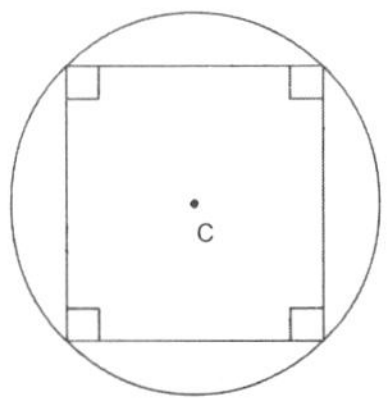

A square inscribed inside a circle can also lead to some interesting problems. The key is to realize that the radius can be drawn to each corner of the square, allowing you to calculate the various areas.

Practice Problems

(1) An isosceles right triangle is inscribed in a circle of radius 6. What is the total area of the the parts of the circle outside the triangle?

(2) An equilateral triangle is inscribed inside a circle of radius 4. What is the area of each of the three wedges outside the triangle but inside the circle?

(3) A square of length 6 is inscribed inside a circle. What is the diameter of the circle? What is the area of each of the 4 wedges outside the square but inside the circle?

7.9 Three-Dimensional Figures

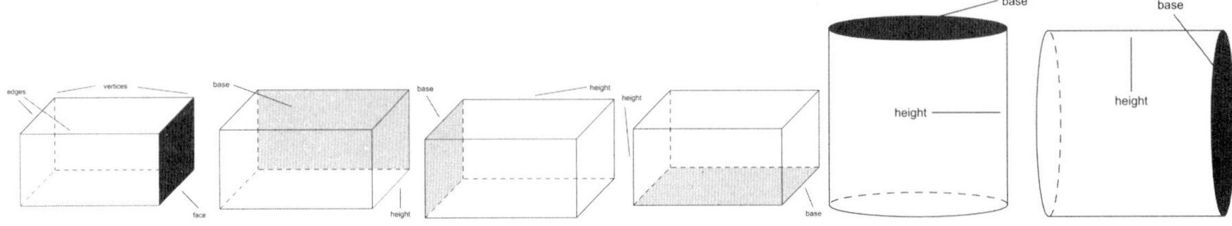

Many people often have difficulty visualizing three-dimensional objects. If you are practicing a particular kind of three-dimensional problem, find a model for that figure (cereal box for the rectangular box, soup can for the cylinder, ball for the sphere) so that you can have something more tangible with which to work.

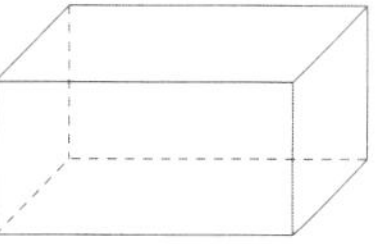

The volume of a rectangular solid is given by $V = lwh$ and the total surface area, assuming all six sides are present (see the cereal box), is given by $A = 2lw + 2lh + 2wh$.

For a cube, which is defined specifically to mean a rectangular solid with each edge having equal length, $V = l^3$ and the surface area is $6l^2$.

Remember to make use of dimensional analysis: you can see here that every volume formula has three units of length being multiplied, giving the three dimensions and every area has two units of length being multiplied, giving the two dimensions. And when calculating perimeters, you can see that each contribution is only one unit of length (1-dimensional).

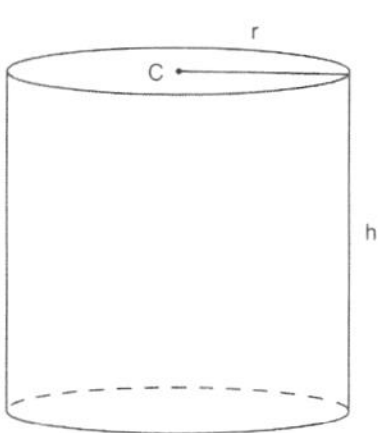

The volume of a cylinder is given by $V = \pi r^2 h$; the surface area depends upon the whether the cylinder has a top, bottom, both or neither. The surface area is $A = 2\pi rh + n\pi r^2$, where n can be 0,1, or 2, depending upon whether there is no top or bottom, a top or a bottom, or both, respectively.

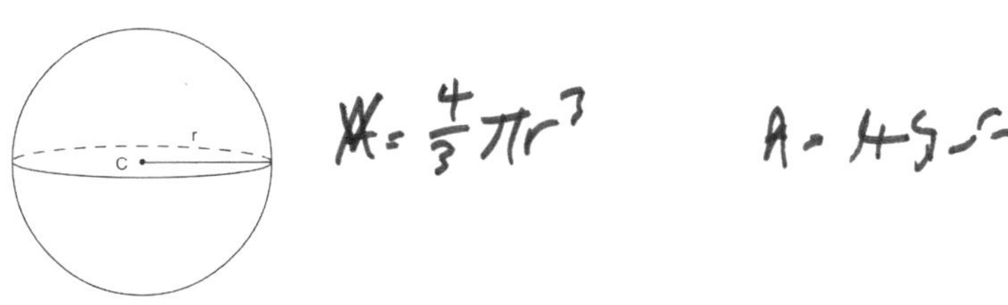

There are no such complications with a sphere. The volume is given by $V = \frac{4}{3}\pi r^3$ and the surface area is $A = 4\pi r^2$.

Practice Problems

(1) A new soft drink company wants to make a can with a cylindrical bottom and a hemispherical (half a sphere) top. If the radius is 3 cm, what does the height of the cylindrical part of the can need to be to give the can a total volume of $99\pi \text{cm}^3$?

(2) If the height of a cylinder is 5, what is the radius at which the volume of a sphere and a cylinder will be the same?

(3) What is the largest volume sphere that will fit completely inside a box of $6 \times 8 \times 10$?

Student Notes:

7.10 Properties of Similar Figures

For similar figures (or objects), *regardless of whether the shapes are irregular*

(1) Any two corresponding lengths are in the *same ratio* as any other pair of corresponding lengths.

(2) Corresponding areas are in the same proportion as the ratio of the *squares* of any of the corresponding lengths.

(3) Corresponding volumes are in the same proportion as the ratio of the *cubes* of any pair of the corresponding lengths.

These elementary relationships have wide-ranging implications, among which is the prediction of the existence of π, used in the computation of the circumference and the area of a circle.

7.11 Extending or Adding Lines

The addition or extension of one or more lines in a given geometrical figure often simplifies the analysis. The aim should be to try to convert the given (unfamiliar) geometrical diagram into a familiar configuration.

Student Notes:

Chapter 8

Word Problems

8.1 Translation

The primary stumbling block for test-takers when encountering word problems is not knowing how to get from the words to the mathematics. The first thing to find out is what you are being asked to find. If it has a dimension, what is it? In other words, if you are being asked to find out how long it takes to do something, how is the time expressed: seconds, minutes, days, etc. Find some way to organize the information in a meaningful and useful way, perhaps graphically or in a table. It should be emphasized that if you know how to do a problem a certain way, go ahead and do it that way. There may be a better way but you will spend more time figuring out how to do it better than you would spend on the problem itself. It is when you are unsure about how to proceed that you need a plan of attack. A *caveat* to maintaining the *status quo* is that if you generally run out of time on the quantitative practice exams, even if you are getting a large fraction correct, your approach will need modification.

The important thing to realize, as you are doing these problems, is not that you are going to do all this work while you are taking the test, but that you are training your brain to organize the information automatically after a while.

Let's look at an example:

Equal amounts of water are poured into jugs of different capacities, filling the larger jar to $\frac{1}{3}$ of its total volume. If the capacity of the smaller jug is $\frac{2}{3}$ of the larger, how full would the smaller jug be if all of the water from the larger were transferred to it?

The two main ideas are drawing a picture and recognizing the word equal. Sketch a couple of jugs with different capacities, recognizing that the larger one must be one-third full. The larger jug has $\frac{3}{2}$ the capacity of the smaller. Therefore, if the larger is one-third full, the smaller must be half full. The amount of water in each is EQUAL, therefore doubling the water in the smaller jug fills it.

Understanding the approach to take is well over half the battle.

Furthermore, when you know will need a certain piece of information but the value has not yet been determined, assign it a variable name and work with it.

Sample Data Sufficiency Question
(Source: GMAT Mini-Test. Reprinted with prior permission.)

Carlotta can drive from her home to her office by one of two possible routes. If she must also return by one of these routes, what is the distance of the shorter route?

(1) When she drives from her home to her office by the shorter route and returns by the longer route, she drives a total of 42 kilometers.

(2) When she drives both ways, from her home to her office and back, by the longer route, she drives a total of 46 kilometers.

- ○ Statement (1) ALONE is sufficient, but statement (2) alone is not sufficient.
- ○ Statement (2) ALONE is sufficient, but statement (1) alone is not sufficient.
- ○ BOTH statements TOGETHER are sufficient, but NEITHER statement ALONE is sufficient.
- ○ EACH statement ALONE is sufficient.
- ○ Statement (1) and (2) TOGETHER are NOT sufficient.

EXPLANATION:

Statement (1) alone is not sufficient because only the sum of the distances of the two routes is given and there are infinitely many pairs of numbers with a given sum.
From (2) the distance of the longer route can be found, but there is no information about the distance of the shorter route. Statement (2) alone is therefore not sufficient.
From (1) and (2) together, the distance of the shorter route can be determined $(42 - 46/2)$, and the third choice is the best.

8.2 Dimensional Analysis

(a) In any equation, the dimensions of the individual terms must be consistent. (It follows then, that if one term in an equation is modified by the addition, substraction, multiplication, and/or division by a dimensional quantity, every other term the equation must be modified in a dimensionally-identical way.) Consider an equation of the form:

$$X = 5A + 3B$$

This equation cannot be simplified or evaluated until the values for A and B are known. Even then, a meaningful value of X cannot be obtained if the quantities, A and B, are not dimensionally *identical.* It is not sufficient for the A and B to be merely dimensionally similar as in the situation where A and B are both lengths but expressed in differing systems of units, e.g., where A might be 3 feet and B equals 2 meters. In such a case, it would be necessary to convert one term into an equivalent length expressed in the other set of units.

With more dissimilar quantities, it may be possible to modify the description of the terms to determine a 'common denominator' where the combination of the terms can be made. If, for example, in the algebraic equation above, if A represented 4 chairs and B represented 2 tables, one could combine the items by noting that both a chair and a table are 'pieces of furniture' and X could be evaluated as:

5(4 chairs) + 3(2 tables) = 20 chairs + 6 tables

$$= 20 \text{ pieces of furniture} + 6 \text{ pieces of furniture}$$
$$= 26 \text{ pieces of furniture}$$

However, in this process of forcing the combination, the constituent details are no longer evident in the answer, i.e., some information is lost.

(b) As long as the *overall* dimensional 'value' of a term matches any other terms added, it is not necessary that individual items in a product of terms have to be dimensionally consistent, e.g., in the expression

$$S = D + VT$$

where S and D are distances, V is speed and T is time, neither V nor T can be dimensionally identical to S or D whereas the product, VT, does have this characteristic. Furthermore, it is always possible to multiply or divide a term by the dimensionless equivalent of 1 in order to convert quantities in one set of units to the equivalent in another set of units, as below:

A man walks D meters in T minutes. In kilometers per hour, the rate at which the man walks is

(A) $\frac{6D}{100T}$ (B) $\frac{6T}{100D}$ (C) $60DT$ (D) $\frac{100D}{6T}$ (E) $\frac{100T}{6D}$

For the problem as stated, a walking speed can be expressed, namely, $R = \frac{D}{T}$, but this expression is in terms of meters per minute, and it is necessary to convert, m/min, into km/hour. To do this, one begins with the valid mathematical statements:

$$1 \text{ km} = 1000 \text{ m} \quad \text{and} \quad 60 \text{ minutes} = 1 \text{ hr}$$

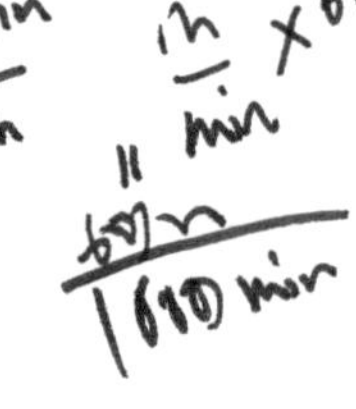

From these the following ratios can be obtained:

$$\frac{60 \text{ minutes}}{1 \text{ hour}} = 1 \qquad \frac{1 \text{ kilometers}}{1000 \text{ meters}} = 1$$

Using these, R becomes:

$$R = \frac{D}{T}(\text{in m/min}) \times \frac{60 \text{ minutes}}{1 \text{ hour}} \times \frac{1 \text{ kilometers}}{1000 \text{ meters}}$$

$$\text{which gives} \quad R = \frac{6\,D}{100\,T} \quad (\text{in km/hr})$$

8.3 Ratio Problems

Let us look at examples.

$\frac{3}{7}$ of a class of students are boys. When the class consists of 91 students, how many are boys?

$$\frac{3}{7} = \frac{x}{91}$$
$$x = 39$$

⇒ Ratio of foreign sales to domestic sales is 4 to 7. How much of the $220 million sales this year is foreign?

$$\frac{4}{7+4} = \frac{x}{220}$$
$$\frac{220}{11} = x$$
$$x = 80$$

In a year there are 200 students, of whom 155 are girls. How many girls have to join so that there are 80% girls?

$$\frac{155 + x}{200 + x} = \frac{8}{10}$$

$$1550 + 10x = 1600 + 8x$$

$$2x = 50$$

$$x = 25$$

Here is a quicker way: 200 students, 155 girls ⇒ 45 boys

45 = 20%
225 = 100%
25 girls have to join

8.4 Rate Problems

Rate problems come in all shapes and sizes, but primarily in three. The overarching theme is that speed multiplied by time equals distance. Here we generalize distance to mean whatever is supposed to be accomplished.

$$Speed \times Time = Distance$$

First Type of Rate Problem

The first kind will involve two participants, operating at different speeds. For example,

A pipe can fill a pool in 5 days. A second pipe can fill the pool in 3 days. Assuming they start working together at the same time, how long will it take to fill the pool if the second pipe stops working after a day?

The key is to realize that this is a speed problem and there are two components: what is being done and what it takes to accomplish the task. The first pipe's speed is $\frac{1}{5}$ pool every day and the second pipe's speed is $\frac{1}{3}$ pool every day. After the first day, $\frac{1}{5} \times 1$ day plus $\frac{1}{3} \times 1$ day results in, after finding the common denominator, $\frac{8}{15}$ of the pool being filled. The remaining $\frac{7}{15}$ of the pool is filled by only the first pipe, $\frac{7}{15} = \frac{1}{5} \times t$, the time needed to fill the rest of the pool, which equals $\frac{7}{3}$ days, for a total of $\frac{10}{3}$ days.

Second Type of Rate Problem

A second kind of problem involves some kind of job and a number of workers needed to complete the task.

It takes ten men 30 days to add a wing to a house. If, when the job is half over, five men are added, what is the total time needed to finish the job?

Again, the job is placed in the numerator, one wing, and what it takes to do the job, ten men 30 days, or 300 man-days, in the denominator. With the original ten men, half the job will be done in 15 days. The next half of the job will also take 150 man-days. But with 15 men, only ten days will be needed, for a total of 25 days.

$$Number\ of\ Workers \times Time = Total\ Job\ Units$$

Third Type of Rate Problem

The third kind typically involves filling a volume:

A barrel of wine is being filled by a worker stepping on grapes. The barrel, with a capacity of 50 liters, is currently one-quarter full. He can step on 500 grapes per minute, each grape a sphere of radius 1 cm, but only yielding seventy-five percent of the volume. How long will it take before the barrel is three-fifths full (Note 1000 cm^3 = 1 liter)?

Working backwards, the difference between three-fifths and one-fourth of 50 liters is $30 - 12.5 = 17.5$ liters. This is what we need to fill. The volume of a sphere is $\frac{4}{3}\pi r^3$, r being the radius of the sphere, in this case 1 cm. Each grape has a volume of $\frac{4}{3}\pi$ cm^3, which translates to $\frac{4\pi}{3000}$ liters. Each minute, the volume created from 500 grapes is $500 \times \frac{4}{3}\pi$ $cm^3 \times \frac{3}{4} = 500\pi$ $cm^3 = \frac{500}{1000}\pi$ liter $= \frac{\pi}{2}$ liter. Now it's just a matter of distance = speed × time, and the number of minutes needed is $17.5/\frac{\pi}{2} = 35/\pi \approx 11$.

More Examples:

Fractional part of job completed = $\frac{time\ worked}{total\ individual\ completion\ time}$

$$\sum_{i=1}^{n} \frac{T}{C_i}$$

Two copy machines can produce a report in 50 and 75 minutes respectively. How long do they take together?

$$\frac{x}{50} + \frac{x}{75} = 1$$

$$\frac{150x}{50} + \frac{150x}{75} = 150$$

$$3x + 2x = 150$$

$$5x = 150$$

$$x = 30$$

Three pipes can fill a tank in 10, 15 and 30 minutes respectively. How long would it take them together?

$$\frac{x}{10} + \frac{x}{15} + \frac{x}{30} = 1$$

$$\frac{30x}{10} + \frac{30x}{15} + \frac{30x}{30} = 30$$

$$3x + 2x + x = 30$$

$$6x = 30$$

$$x = 5$$

Two copy machines can produce a report together in 16 minutes. If one machine is twice as fast as the other, how long would it take the slower machine to completer the job alone?

$$\frac{16}{x} + \frac{16}{2x} = 1$$

$$16 + 8 = x$$

$$x = 24$$

$$2x = 48$$

8.5 Exponential Growth

A common kind of problem involves the growth of something such that it doubles, triples, what have you every certain unit of time. For example, a city has a population of 1 million people and the population is doubling every 20 years. In how many years will the population grow to 16 million? Step by step, you see that in twenty years, the population will be 2 million. Twenty years later, the population will be 4 million. Twenty years later, 8 million, and twenty years later again, 16 million, for a total of 80 years.

The formula should look something like the following:

$$F = Ia^{n/t}$$

$16 = 1 \times 2^{n/20}$

$16 = 2^{n/20}$

where F is the final value (in the example above, the population of 16 million), I is the initial value (the starting value of 1 million), a is the growth factor (in this case 2, because the population is doubling), t is the number of periods that it takes for the growth to reach the first factor (in this case twenty years), and n is the total number of time periods needed, which was 80 years, 4 times 20 years.

The formula can be rearranged to allow you to solve for the value you are seeking. This should also be familiar because it is the same concept as compound interest, where the growth of your money in the bank relies on earning interest on the interest. In the example above, the continued doubling relied on the doubling of the newcomers to the city.

It is also very useful to draw a timeline. Starting with time 0, make a tick mark and above fill in the initial value. For every time period, make another tick mark and each time multiply by the growth factor until you reach the desired result.

Practice Problems

(1) A certain bacterium in a Petri dish triples every 12 hours. When the biologist left for the weekend, there were 10,000 bacteria in the dish. How many were there when she came back, Monday morning, 60 hours later?

(2) You have a virus but are recovering. Right now, two million cells are infected. To be healthy, fewer than 200,000 need to be infected. The number of infected cells halves every 4 hours. After about how long will you be healthy?

(3) The number of people applying to business schools is growing exponentially (not really), such that every 15 years, the number of applicants doubles. As a result, admissions rates are falling such that every 15 years, the acceptance rate halves. Columbia's is about 8 %. When will it be 1 %?

Student Notes:

8.6 Questions with Missing Information

If faced with a question that appears to require additional information before it can be solved, there must be three possibilities:

(1) You have misunderstood the question.

(2) The problem has been correctly interpreted and more data is needed to solve it. If this is the case, one if the choices will contain a statement to reflect this. However, if the all choices given are specific in nature, then this possibility can be ruled out.

(3) Additional information is not needed to solve the problem.

If the last possibility is the case, then the problem can be solved by using numerical values and/or simplifying the geometry, consistent with the problem. Two examples below are taken from past questions:

A computer is programmed to add 2 to a number X, multiply the result by 2, subtract 2 and divide the result by 2. The computers answer will be:

(A) $X - 1$ (B) X (C) $X + \frac{1}{2}$ (D) $X + 1$ (E) $X + 2$

In this case, the problem does not specify a value for X, and consequently, the solution must be valid for any value of X. A value of X should be chosen that allows an answer to be worked out from the question and this result compared to the values obtained by using the same value of X in the choices offered. Similarly, in the geometry example:

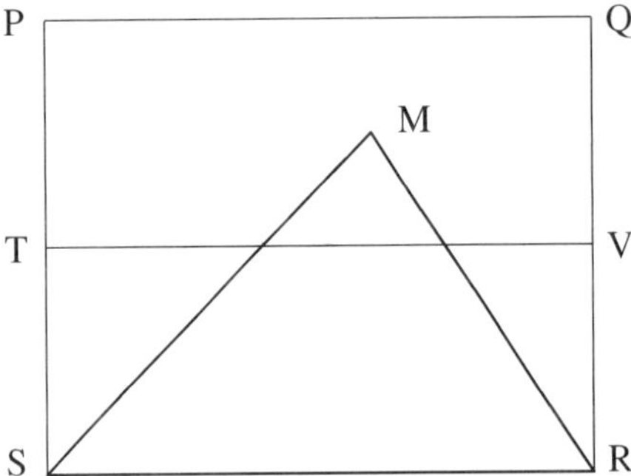

The area of rectangle PQRS is 48, QV = VR, and PT = TS. If point M is somewhere inside rectangle PQVT, and if x is the area of the triangle MRS, which of the following includes the only possible values of area x?

(A) $6 < x < 24$ (B) $12 < x < 24$ (C) $12 < x < 48$
(D) $24 < x < 48$ (E) $48 < x < 96$

This problem can be solved by assuming values for the vertical and horizontal lengths of rectangle PQRS consistent with the area of the rectangle being 48, e.g., using values such as 6 and 8, or 4 and 12. Another approach would be to recognize that since M could be anywhere within PQVT, point M could be nearly coincident with either point V (below, left) or point Q (below, right).

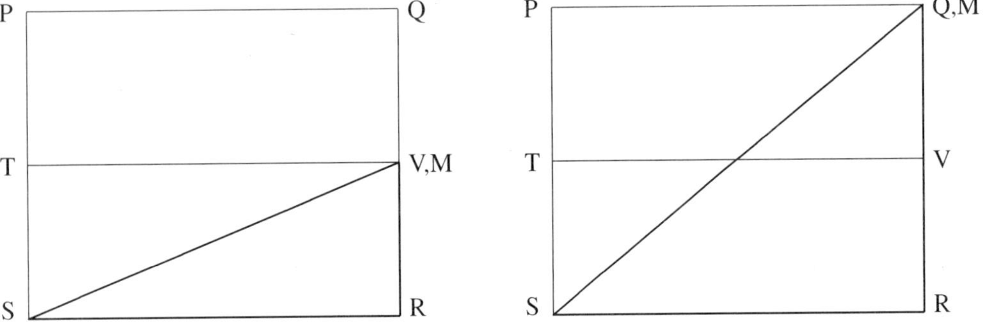

For these two cases, it becomes clear that the area of MRS must be half the area of rectangles TVRS which itself is half of the area of PQRS. Thus, in the left diagram, x must equal $\frac{1}{2}$ of $\frac{1}{2}$ of 48, or 12. In the right diagram, the area of MRS must be half the area of PQRS, i.e., $\frac{1}{2}$ of 48, or 24.

Student Notes:

8.7 Mixtures

In problems involving mixtures or the changing of the properties of the constituents, if the problem consists of adding a pure constituent to some mixture, it is generally easier to work with the component that does *not* change.

Student Notes:

$\frac{2(x+2)-2}{2}$ $x+1$

Student Notes:

Chapter 9

Statistics

9.1 Sets

For the purposes of the GMAT, a set is a group of numbers brought together for a particular reason. For example, perhaps, given a class of 6 students, we wanted to know the number of questions each answered correctly on a GMAT diagnostic test. The set might be 28, 17, 22, 19, 23, 23. Each entry represents someone's score. Notice that there are two 23's. That is fine. It simply means that two different people each scored 23 on the test.

9.2 Arithmetic Mean

For the set in question, suppose we wanted to calculate the mean. Add the scores together and divide by the number of scores we have. $\frac{28+17+22+19+23+23}{6} = \frac{132}{6} = 22$. This is how the mean is calculated.

The formula is as follows:

$\bar{x} = \frac{1}{n}\sum_i^n x_i$

where x_i is the ith element of the set.

9.2.1 Determining Averages

Determining the average of a set of numbers is a calculation we all carry out regularly, most often by adding the individual values together and dividing the result by the number of items being averaged. The method suggested below keeps the computations within the realm of small numbers thus increasing the speed of computation while reducing the probability of making errors. To find the average:

(1) Assume an approximate value of the average to be calculated

(2) Determine the deviation of each value from the assumed average

(3) Average the deviations obtained

(4) Add the average deviation to the assumed average

For example, to find the average of six scores, 73, 87, 63, 68, 79 and 75, one might choose 70 as an approximate average. This choice will give the following deviations

score	deviation
73	+3
87	+17
68	-2
62	-8
79	+9
75	+5
sum	+24

Adding the deviations produces +24, dividing by 6 gives +4. Adding this last value to the assumed average, 70, gives 70 + 4 or 74 as the actual average.

It should be noted that the magnitudes of the deviations depend only on the spread of the original values and not on the actual size of these values. If the example above had been to find the average of six numbers that were exactly 6,300 units greater than the problem given, i.e., 6,373, 6,387, 6,368, etc., the choice of an assumed average of 6,370 would have given rise to exactly the same list of deviations listed above.

What's the average of 763, 781, 758, 777 and 775?

$$\begin{aligned} 763 - 770 &= -7 \\ 781 - 770 &= 11 \\ 758 - 770 &= -12 \\ 777 - 770 &= 7 \\ 775 - 770 &= 5 \end{aligned}$$

$$-7 + 11 - 12 + 7 + 5 = 4$$

$$770 + \frac{4}{5} = 770.8$$

Assume at a weather station the temperature is measured on 6 consecutive days. The first 5 are known and the average is 28C. The question is what value was observed on the last day?

$$20, 33, 23, 30, 27$$

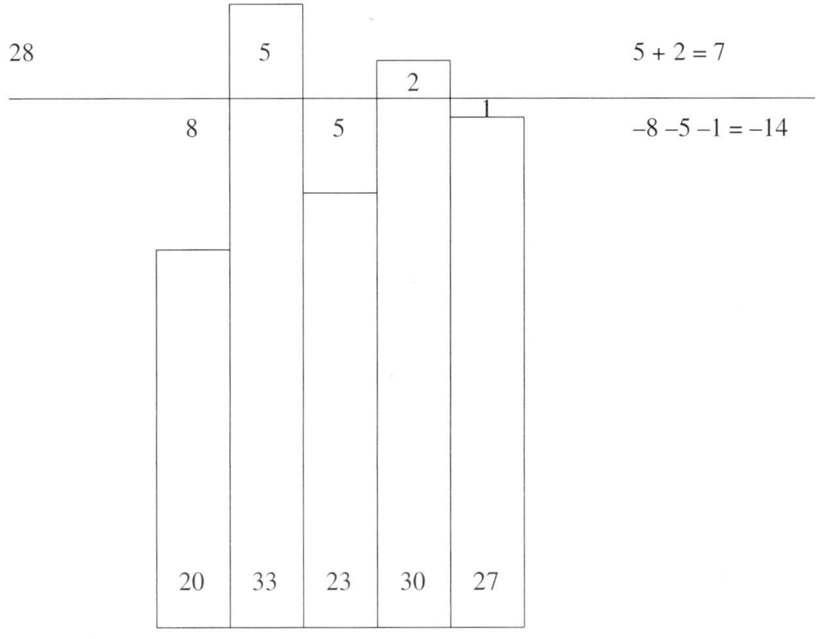

$$28 + 7 = 35$$

Please remember that the average of a set of consecutive integers is the *middle number*. The same rule holds true for any set in which the terms are space evenly apart.

4, 6, 8, 10, 12 ⇒ Average: 8
11, 19, 27, 35, 43 ⇒ Average: 27

9.3 Mode

The mode is the element in the set that appears the most often. In our case, the mode is 23. Note that as long as there are elements in the set, it will have a mode. There may be more than one. In fact, if we changed our set slightly, 28, 17, 22, 19, 23, 21, this set would have 6 modes (the set would be hexamodal). But our original set has one mode (unimodal).

9.4 Median

To calculate the median for our original set, we have to do a little bit of work first. We need to arrange the elements from least to greatest, left to right. 17, 19, 22, 23, 23, 28 would be how it would look. If we had an odd number of elements, we would just pick the one in the middle. Since we have an even number, however, add the two in the middle and divide by 2, $\frac{22+23}{2} = 22.5$ would be the median.

9.5 Range

To calculate the range, find the difference between the largest and the smallest elements in the set (the difference between the element farthest to the right on the number line and the element farthest to the left. $28 - 17 = 11$ is the range. It gives us an impression of how far apart the elements are.

9.6 Standard Deviation

Standard deviation is among the more difficult concepts tested on the GMAT. It gives us a more precise notion of the average distance of each element from the mean. What does this mean? We saw that the mean is 22. But we also know that not everyone scored 22 on the test, so there must be a spread around the mean. The standard deviation measures this spread. The larger the standard deviation, the larger the spread.

This point is best seen by comparison. Suppose we had 6 other students take the diagnostic test. Their scores were 20, 21, 22, 22, 23, 24. Here the mean is also 22 but you see that the spread among the scores is much smaller, meaning that the standard deviation is smaller as well.

It is exceedingly rare to actually need to calculate the standard deviation but just in case, the formula looks like this (σ represents the standard deviation):

$$\sigma = \sqrt{\frac{\sum_{i=1}^{n}(x_i - \bar{x})^2}{n}}$$

What does all this mean? The $\sum_{i=1}^{n}$ means we are summing over each element to the number of elements n. In our case, the number of elements $n = 6$. The x_i refers to the ith element. For example, if i were 1, we would be referring to the first element. The $\bar{x}$ refers to the mean. In our case, taking the original set, we would calculate

$$\sigma = \sqrt{\frac{(17-22)^2+(19-22)^2+(22-22)^2+(23-22)^2+(23-22)^2+(28-22)^2}{6}}$$

The next step

$$\sigma = \sqrt{\frac{(-5)^2+(-3)^2+(0)^2+(1)^2+(1)^2+(6)^2}{6}}$$

Next,

$$\sigma = \sqrt{\frac{25+9+0+1+1+36}{6}} = \sqrt{\frac{72}{6}} = \sqrt{12} = 2\sqrt{3}$$

If we do the same for the second set we were comparing, we would get a standard deviation of $\sqrt{\frac{5}{3}}$, and as we previously thought, a much smaller spread.

We simply started with the first term, subtracted the mean from it, squared the result, added all the results for each term, divided by the number of terms, then took the square root.

Practice Problems

(1) Find the mean, mode, median, range, and standard deviation for the following sets:

  (a) $\{2, 5, 8, 11, 17, 20\}$

  (b) $\{-3, 0, 6, 6, 9\}$

(2) Given a set $\{3, 5, 16, 22, x\}$, what does x have to be for the mean of the set to be 10?

Student Notes:

$$\sqrt{\frac{\sum (x_i - \bar{x})^2}{n}} = \sigma$$

$$\frac{3 + 5 + 16 + 22 + x}{5} = 10$$

$$50 = 3 + 5 + 16 + 22 + x$$

$$x = 4$$

Chapter 10

Combinatorics

10.1 The Basic Idea

Combinatorics is a fancy word for counting. The problems can be relatively simple (How many different license plates can be made if the license plate needs to have 2 letters and 3 numbers, in that order?) or much more complicated (How many ways can a straight flush be dealt if two of the cards originally dealt must be discarded and replaced, but not if all 5 cards are clubs?). We could go on. But that would not be on the GMAT.

As you are working through one of these counting problems, it is often best to attempt to visualize the situation by drawing a picture. Let's take the first question, for example. We have 5 spaces to fill. The first two are to have letters in them and the last three to have digits. 26 letters in the alphabet means we can put 26 possible things in the first space and 26 in the second space. Ten digits (0-9) means we can put 10 possible numbers in the third, 10 in the fourth, and 10 in the fifth space. So the total is $26 \times 26 \times 10 \times 10 \times 10 = (26)^2(10)^3$. It is very important to be aware of how the answers are expressed in the question to avoid any unnecessary computation.

On the other hand, what if the letters and the digits cannot be repeated? Then the first space could house 26 letters and the second space 25. The first slot for the digits could hold 10, the second 9, and the last 8. The total would then be $26 \times 25 \times 10 \times 9 \times 8$. As in probability, the idea of replacement has a strong influence on the nature of the problem.

Practice Problems

(1) A new country needs to create a flag and has decided upon a three-stripe design. It has five colors to choose from: blue, green, yellow, white, and red, and no color can be used more than once. How many different flags can be created?

(2) A game is being played with a die. The die is rolled three times and each roll recorded. How many different arrangements are possible? What if previously rolled numbers do not count?

(3) You have four friends in town but only two extra tickets for the concert. How many ways can the tickets be distributed if you want to keep at least two friends?

(4) On a one-day expedition to Manhattan, the tour guide asks you to choose from among five restaurants for breakfast, ten for lunch, and twenty for dinner. How many different restaurant combinations can be created?

10.2 Permutations

There are situations where the orientation of the arrangement matters and those when it does not. Looking back at the practice problems, if the country's flag were red, blue, and green, left to right, a different flag would be created if red and blue were switched. On the other hand, if the two people you took with you to the concert switched tickets, the same two people would still be going to the concert.

In the flag problem, order matters. In problems such as that one where if you switch two members of the arrangement and get a different arrangement, that is called a permutation. Trip itineraries, where if you change the order of the cities visited, the itinerary must change, are examples of permutations. Arranging books on a bookshelf is another. Switching the order of the books on the shelf does create a new arrangement.

There are a couple of approaches to doing these kinds of problems. The one you use will likely depend on your comfort level with remembering formulae. The different approaches are best illuminated by using an example and showing how they come to the same conclusion.

Suppose you have enrolled in business school and have purchased one book for each of your five classes. You have one shelf to put them on. How many different arrangements are possible?

The first way involves sketching the situation.

—- —- —- —- —-

Each book must find its appropriate slot. How many books can be placed in the first slot? 5. The second? 4. The third? 3. The fourth? 2. And the fifth? 1.

$5 \times 4 \times 3 \times 2 \times 1 = 5! = 120$

The 'exclamation mark' is here called the factorial sign, where

$n! = n \times (n-1) \times (n-2) \ldots 3 \times 2 \times 1$

The formulaic approach is to say that I have five things to choose from and five places to put them.

${}_5P_5 = \frac{5!}{(5-5)!} = \frac{5!}{0!} = 5!/1 = 5! = 120$

By definition, $0! = 1$. The table below gives the values for the integers from 0 to 7. If a problem involves factorials of a larger number, the answer will be left in factorial form, rather than multiplied out. The GMAT is not solely a test of your multiplication abilities.

n	0	1	2	3	4	5	6	7
$n!$	1	1	2	6	24	120	720	5040

The general formula for arranging k objects when you have n to choose from (when order matters) is

${}_nP_k = \frac{n!}{(n-k)!}$.

For example, what if there were only space on the shelf for three books?

—- —- —-

Again, five could be put in the first slot, four in the second, and three in the third. But that is it. $5 \times 4 \times 3 = 60$.

Using the formula,

${}_5P_3 = \frac{5!}{(5-3)!} = \frac{5!}{2!} = \frac{5 \times 4 \times 3 \times 2 \times 1}{2 \times 1} = 5 \times 4 \times 3 = 60$

Practice Problems

(1) How many different possible combinations can a combination lock have if 35 numbers are available and the combination is 3 numbers long, with no number being repeated? Does order matter?

(2) On a museum wall, there are five places to hang paintings and ten paintings to choose from. How many different arrangements are possible?

(3) At the finals of the 100-meter dash, there are 8 contestants. The top three finishers will be given their metals atop the podium. In how many different ways could the medals be distributed, assuming no ties?

10.3 Combinations

When does order not matter? When putting together teams, counting possible hands in poker, and similar situations. This changes the visualization and calculation process slightly. The following two examples illustrate the difference between permutations (when order matters) and combinations (when order does not):

You have seven candidates and four job vacancies to fill: analyst, consultant, programmer, and engineer. How many different ways can these four positions be filled? As before, you have seven people to choose from to fill the analyst slot, six then to fill the consultant slot, five to fill the programmer slot, and four left for the engineer's position.

$_7P_4 = \frac{7!}{(7-4)!} = 7 \times 6 \times 5 \times 4 = 840$

Note that if you switch two people you have created a different arrangement because people will have different jobs.

Now suppose you have seven candidates and four job vacancies but each vacancy is an analyst position at the same firm. If you switch two people around, you have changed nothing because they are still analysts. Instead of 4! arrangements of four people in four different positions, there is just one arrangement, because no matter how you mix up the four analysts, nothing changes. In this case, we need to divide by 4! to avoid overcounting. When the jobs are indistinguishable, the number of arrangements becomes

$_7C_4 = \frac{7!}{(7-4)!4!} = \frac{7\times6\times5\times4}{4\times3\times2\ times1} = 7 \times 5 = 35$

The general formula for arranging k objects when you have n to choose from (when order does not matter) is

$_nC_k = \frac{n!}{(n-k)!k!}$

where the additional $k!$ in the denominator comes from the fact that switching two objects within the arrangement changes nothing.

Practice Problems

(1) How many different teams of 4 consultants can be formed if the project manager has 8 to choose from?

(2) A tennis tournament begins with 16 players. How many different arrangements are possible for the semi-finals?

(3) To make a co-ed volleyball team, you need three men and three women. If your company has 6 men and 5 women who want to play, how many different teams can be made?

10.4 Identical Objects

One kind of twist that can be put on combinatorics problems is to specify that some of the objects are identical. Suppose you switched two of the identical objects. The two arrangements are indistinguishable and are hence the same. To help elucidate this concept, we return to a simplified version of the flag problem. If we had originally only three colors to choose from, we would have been able to create 3! = 6 flags. If those colors were all identical, we would have been able to make one flag, since rearranging identical stripes does not at all change the appearance.

There are two basic ways the problem can be arranged: either arranging different kinds of identical items (for example, blue pencils and red pencils) or arranging some number of identical items in a different number of slots (for example, 5 peanut butter sandwiches in 8 lunchboxes). The formula for the first situation looks like: the number of arrangments is given by

$$\frac{n!}{k_1!k_2!...k_n!}$$

where n is the total number of objects and k_i is the number of objects of the ith kind. Suppose you had 4 identical red shirts, 3 identical blue shirts, and 2 identical white shirts. How many different ways could you arrange them in your closet? You have 9 shirts total so the number of arrangements would be

$$\frac{9!}{4!3!2!} = \frac{9\times8\times7\times6\times5}{3\times2\times2} = 1260.$$

The second kind of question is just a restatement of a combination question; in the case of the peanut butter sandwiches, you are merely arranging 5 boxes with peanut butter sandwiches and 3 without. This is exactly the same as the combinations formula:

$$\frac{8!}{5!3!} = \frac{8\times7\times6}{3\times2} = 56$$

Because as before, order does not matter. Either you get a peanut butter sandwich or you do not. Either you are on the team or you are not. Either you get the card in your hand or you do not. It is all the same.

Practice Problems

(1) Suppose you are Andy Warhol's assistant and you have generated 10 prints of an iPod: 4 in red, 3 in blue, 2 in green, and one in chartreuse. Andy says that the prints need to be arranged in a horizontal row. How many distinguishable ways can it be done?

(2) The company you work for will, in exchange for your slaving through lunch and dinner, pay for three of your lunches and two of your dinners each week. Friday night, you are never in the office and you refuse to work weekends. How many different ways can you utilize this perk?

10.5 Circular Arrangements

A classic question is to ask how many ways can you seat n guests at a circular dinner table. The key is to realize that if everyone stood up and moved one chair to the left, the arrangement would be unchanged. Each person would still be seated across from the same person he was previously. And you could do this n times.

The number of ways to arrange n non-identical things in a circle is therefore, $(n-1)!$. The more general approach is to take one thing as an anchor for every circular arrangement and arrange everything else around the anchor.

Suppose for example, you were hosting a dinner party for 6, including yourself, three men and three women. How many ways could you arrange the seating such that it was boy, girl, boy, girl, boy, girl. As always, drawing the picture is very helpful. Start counting. There are three possibilities for the person sitting next to you, two for the next seat over, two for the one after that, and one each for the final two seats. $3\times2\times2\times1\times1 = \frac{3!3!}{3} = 12$. For the general case, with n men and women each, the number of possibilities is $n!(n-1)!$, NOT $(n-1)!(n-1)!$. Remember you only need *one* anchor for each circular arrangement.

Practice Problems

(1) How many ways can 5 keys be arranged on a key chain?

(2) A design for a new roulette wheel uses the numbers 1 - 20. How many arrangements can be made if the numbers must alternate odd and even? Leave the answer in terms of factorials.

10.6 Advanced Topics

The more advanced combinatorics problems involve constraints or arrangements within arrangements. An example of a problem involving a constraint might look like: You have a group project which needs to be split into two different parts. Each part will be worked on by three people but two of the group members refuse to work with each other. How many different possible ways are there to arrange the two groups of three? It is an ordinary combinations problem except that a wrinkle has been added.

The approach to take is to begin by solving the base case (the case with no constraint). If nothing else, if you can solve the base case, it may be that some of the answer choices exceed the number for the base case. You can eliminate those as possibilities as the constraint must reduce the possibilities. The base case answer is 20 (we'll let you figure out why; how do you arrange 2 teams of three from a group of 6?). The constraint cannot be dealt with formulaically; this is when logic and some reasoning take place.

If our 6 group members are A, B, C, D, E, and F, ABC ABD ABE ABF ACD ACE ACF ADE ADF AEF BCD BCE BCF BDE BDF BEF CDE CDF CEF DEF are the twenty possibilities.

Let's assume that A and B are on the same team. Then we can subtract those possibilities containing both A and B or neither A and B from the base case of twenty possibilities. How many those possibilities are there? A, B, and blank: blank to be filled in by C, D, E, or F. 4. For neither, we have 4 possibilities for three slots: ${}_4C_3 = 4$. $20 - 4 - 4 = 12$.

Notice that if the projects were the same, there would only be 10 arrangements for the base case and 6 for the AB restrictive case because ABC working on one is equivalent to DEF working on the other, if the two projects are identical.

A second type of advanced problem concerns arrangements within arrangements. For example, 3 couples go together to a Broadway show and have 6 consecutive seats. How many different ways can it be arranged so that each couple sits together? If there were no such constraint, it would be 6!, so there will be fewer possibilities. The key is to treat each couple as a unit, leaving three units to be arranged. So we get a factor of 3!. But each couple can sit in two ways, BG or GB. And there are three couples, giving a factor of 2^3. The result must therefore be $3!2^3 = 48$.

The general approach is to find the number of units n and then the number of degrees of freedom within each type of unit.

Practice Problems

(1) Three countries each send 6 diplomats to a state dinner. The dinner table is arranged into three sections, one for each country. How many ways can all diplomats be seated while each country's diplomats are all seated in the same section? Keep the answer expressed in terms of factorials.

(2) How many ways can a group of 10 friends, among them 3 couples, sit in 10 connected seats at a movie theater, so that each couple can stay together?

(3) A country's flag needs 5 vertical stripes. The colors are to be red, green, blue, white, and yellow, with each color used exactly once. How many different arrangements are there if green and yellow cannot be adjacent?

Student Notes:

5!

4! $4 \times 3 \times 2 = 24$

$20!$ $(19!)$

personal
academic
professional experience

2 parts
3 people each (6)

$\frac{6!}{3!3!} = \frac{6 \times 5 \times 4}{3 \times 2} = 20$

commitments

careers

$3!\,2^3 = 48$

1) $3! \times 6! \times 6! \times 6!$

2) $7!\,2^3$

3) $5!$ $\quad 4! \times 2 \quad 4 \times 3 \times 2 \times 2$ (48)

$5 \times 4 \times 3 \times 2$

$120 - 48 = 72$

Chapter 11

Probability

11.1 The Basic Idea

The probability of something happening is given by the number of ways that particular something can happen divided by the number of ways that anything can happen. Paradoxically, the difficulty of these problems lies in counting. What does that mean?

To take an extremely simple example, the probability of rolling a '3' with a fair 6-sided die is $\frac{1}{6}$, because there are 6 evenly weighted possibilities of rolling different numbers and '3' is one of them.

We counted 6 equally weighted possibilities for the die and we counted 1 for which we were looking. Hence, $\frac{1}{6}$.

A more difficult example would be: A slightly inebriated darts player takes aim at the dartboard. His probability of making the dart stick in one of the twenty possible numbers is $\frac{1}{25}$, each number equally likely. His probability of hitting a bull's-eye is $\frac{1}{100}$. What is his probability of hitting a two-digit prime number? The solution is merely a matter of counting, as all these questions are. What are the two-digit prime numbers? 11, 13, 17, 19. Each of these will occur with a probability of $\frac{1}{25}$, making the probability $\frac{4}{25}$.

What if the question had been: What is the probability of not hitting the board at all? The probability of something happening must be 1. In other words, something has to happen, hitting a number, the bull's-eye, or missing the board entirely. There are no other possibilities. The probabilities, therefore, must sum to 1. $20 \cdot \frac{1}{25} + \frac{1}{100} + x = 1$, where x is the probability of missing entirely. Solving for x, we conclude that the probability of missing entirely is $\frac{19}{100}$.

The key lies in knowing that something must happen; the sum of all the probabilities must be 1. If you count all the probabilities and get something other than 1, either you counted incorrectly or you did not consider all the possibilities.

Practice Problems

(1) What is the probability of rolling '7' with two fair six-sided dice? An '11'?

(2) Assuming it is equally likely to dial any particular digit on a telephone, what is the probability that the first digit dialed is an odd prime number?

(3) What is the probability of drawing a numbered card from a standard deck of 52 playing cards?

11.2 Terminology

Within the previous section, there was an implicit (and true) assumption built in: the different possible occurrences were *mutually exclusive*. In other words, you could not roll a '3' at the same time as a '5' with the six-sided die. The darts player could not miss the board entirely and still hit the bull's-eye. You cannot flip a coin and get heads and tails at the same time. In a more mathematical notation, two events, A and B, are mutually exclusive if $P(A \cap B) = 0$. In words, this equation says that the probability of A *and* B must be zero if the events are mutually exclusive.

Complementarity occurs when exactly one of the events delineated *must* occur. For example, when a coin is flipped, it must either land heads or tails. When a die is rolled, the number must either be even or odd. These are complementary events. Mathematically, if two events, A and B, are complementary, $P(A \cup B) = 1$. The probability of A *or* B is 1. Note that complementarity does not necessarily imply mutual exclusivity. For example, all the cars in a parking lot could be either SUVs or red. This does not exclude the possibility of having a red SUV.

To illustrate your understanding of a problem, often times you can use various *Venn diagrams* to make it easier to follow.

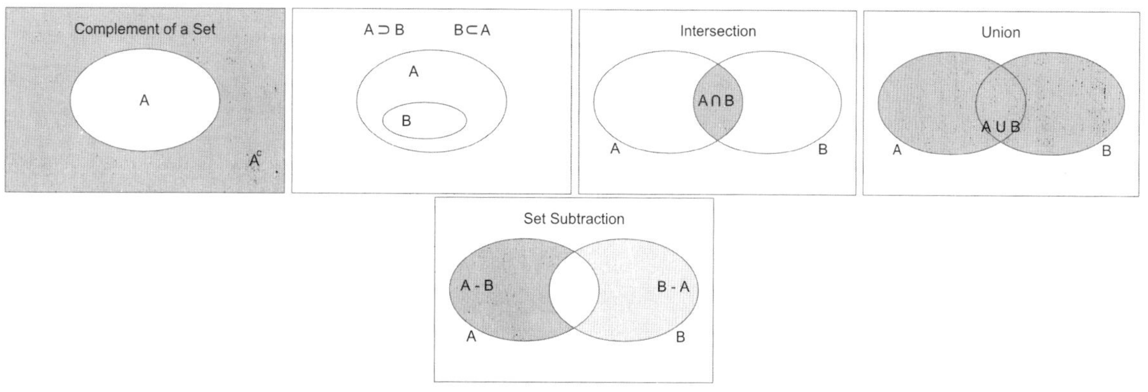

Practice Problems

Are the following events complementary, mutually exclusive, both, or neither?

(1) Red or Black on a roulette wheel

(2) Red or Black when picking a card out the standard 52-card deck

(3) Rejection by or Admission to the business school of your choice

(4) Weather: Rain or Shine

(5) Weather: Hot or Cold

11.3 Dependent and Independent Events

Dependent and independent events are terms that talk about probabilities in terms of sequence, meaning that the question is whether the outcome of the prior events influences the result of following events.

To illustrate independent events, think about flipping a coin. Suppose a fair coin is tossed ten times and the first nine times it lands on heads. What is the probability of landing on tails the tenth time? $\frac{1}{2}$. It does not matter what happened the first nine times. The events are independent. Each coin flip is independent of previous coin flips. Each roll of a die is independent of previous die rolls. When events are independent, $P(A \cap B) = P(A)P(B)$, by extension $P(A \cap B \cap C) = P(A)P(B)P(C)$, and so on.

On the other hand, let's look at another example for the gamblers among you. What is the probability of drawing an ace from a standard deck of 52 cards? $\frac{4}{52} = \frac{1}{13}$. What about the second draw? Does it matter what happened the first time? Suppose we know that we did not draw an ace the first time. Then the probability must be the number of aces left in the deck divided by the number of cards left in the deck: $\frac{4}{51}$. If an ace was drawn the first time, however, then the number of aces left is 3 and the number of cards left is 51: the probability becomes $\frac{3}{51} = \frac{1}{17}$. So it clearly matters what happened the first time. And if we do not know what happened the first time? Then we must consider both possibilities, drawing an ace the first time and not drawing an ace the first time. The probability of not drawing an ace the first time is $\frac{12}{13}$ so the probability of drawing an ace the second time, when we do not know what we drew the first time is: $P(A_1)P_{A_1}(A_2) + P(/A_1)P_{/A_1}(A_2) = \frac{1}{13}\frac{1}{17} + \frac{12}{13}\frac{4}{51}$. And after doing the math, we find that the probability is $\frac{1}{13}$. So if we do not know what we drew the first time, the probability of drawing an ace the second time is exactly the same. If we do know, however, then everything changes. Furthermore, the probability of drawing an ace on the 52nd draw, if we do not know what happened on the first 51... the calculation is significantly longer but the answer is still $\frac{1}{13}$.

With dependent events, $P(A \cap B) = P(B)P_B(A) = P(A)P_A(B)$. In words, the probability of A and B occurring is the probability of B multiplied by the probability of A given that B has occurred or the probability of A multiplied by the probability of B given that A has occurred.

One last point:

When problems talk about 'with replacement,' that implies that the events are independent because whatever was taken was then put back, restoring the original conditions. When a problem talks about 'without replacement,'that implies that the events are dependent because the conditions have changed because the item pulled out has not been replaced.

Practice Problems

(1) Will the probability of throwing a '6' on a six-sided die depend on what the previous throw was? So then what is the probability of throwing two 'sixes' in a row?

(2) What is the probability of getting three heads in a row when tossing a fair coin?

(3) Suppose you forgot your 4-digit PIN number for your ATM card. Does the probability of guessing correctly depend on how many previous combinations you have tried?

(4) What is the probability of drawing two kings in a row if the first card is not replaced?

(5) An urn contains 20 balls, 10 black and 10 white. What is the probability of drawing one black and one white ball, when the first ball taken out is not replaced? When it is replaced?

11.4 Two Overlapping Events

Suppose we want to find the probability of something occurring with multiple properties. For example, the probability of drawing a red face card from a standard deck of 52 playing cards. We could approach this problem in one of two ways. First, how many face cards are there? Jack, Queen, and King in four different suits for a total of 12. Of these four suits, how many are red? Two. There should be 6 (3×2) red face cards and 52 cards to choose from, so the probability is $\frac{6}{52} = \frac{3}{26}$. Or, how many red cards are there? 26. How many of these are face cards? 6. Either way we computed it, we did the following: we looked at one of the conditions (face card or red) and from there, calculated how many that satisfied the first condition also satisfied the second. Mathematically, the probability of event A and B is given by $P(A \cap B) = P(B)P_B(A) = P(A)P_A(B)$, where $P_A(B)$ is the probability of B occurring given that A has occurred. Another way, and typically simpler, is simply to count the number of cards that have both qualities and divide by the total number of cards to find the probability.

What about the probability of drawing a red card *or* a face card? We know the probability of drawing a red card is $\frac{1}{2}$. We know the probability of drawing a face card is $\frac{12}{52} = \frac{3}{13}$. But from the previous example, we also know that there is some overlap. It means that if we try simply to add the two probabilities, we will have overestimated the probability. Looking at the Venn diagram, we see that we would have added $P(A \cap B)$ twice. Thus, we need to subtract the intersection to avoid double counting.

$P(A \cup B) = P(A) + P(B) - P(A \cap B)$

And in this case, $\frac{1}{2} + \frac{3}{13} - \frac{3}{26} = \frac{32}{52} = \frac{8}{13}$.

Practice Problems

(1) What is the probability of drawing a black, even-numbered card from the standard deck?

(2) What is the probability of drawing a king or a black card?

(3) Two credit card companies have sent you applications in the mail. You know that the probability of being accepted by one or the other is 100%, the probability of acceptance by the first is 70%, and the probability of being accepted by both is 30%. What is the probability of acceptance by the second company?

11.5 Three Overlapping Events

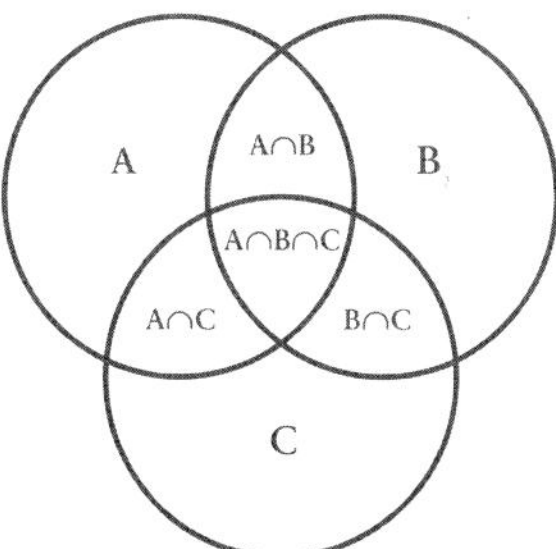

The likelihood of seeing a problem involving three dependent events is small but it is not zero and seeing the extrapolation to three should enhance the understanding of problems involving two dependent events.

This is seen from the equation:

$P(A \cup B \cup C) = P(A) + P(B) + P(C) - P(A \cap B) - P(A \cap C) - P(B \cap C) + P(A \cap B \cap C)$

Taking this calculation step by step, and looking at the figure, we see that when we add $P(A) + P(B) + P(C)$, we have overcounted the intersections $P(A \cap B)$, $P(A \cap C)$, and $P(B \cap C)$. So we subtract those. But then we undercounted $P(A \cap B \cap C)$ and must put that back. From this, we get the preceding result.

Another way of viewing the problem of three overlapping events would be to break the probabilities up into a probability of only one event of the three occuring, exactly two of the events occurring, and all three of the events occurring:

$P(A \cup B \cup C) = P(A \cap \bar{B} \cap \bar{C}) + P(B \cap \bar{A} \cap \bar{C}) + P(C \cap \bar{A} \cap \bar{B}) +$
$P(A \cap B \cap \bar{C}) - P(A \cap C \cap \bar{B}) - P(B \cap C \cap \bar{A}) +$
$P(A \cap B \cap C)$

where $\bar{A}$ means everything outside of A.

Three first three terms added together give the probability of exactly one of the events occurring, the second three exactly two, and the last the probability of all three.

Practice Problems

(1) A car dealership has 50 cars in the showroom. The probability of a car being red is 40%, the probability of it being a convertible is 30%, and the probability of it being a hybrid is 20%. The probability of it being red, a convertible, or a hybrid is 48%. The probability that it is a red convertible is 20%, the probability that it is a convertible hybrid is 10%, and the probability that it is a red hybrid is 16%. How many red, convertible hybrids are in the showroom?

11.6 Test Taking Hints

Not only is the concept of complementarity one of the most important concepts in understanding probability, it is also extremely useful in the actual test-taking process. The reason is because the GMAT is a multiple-choice test. If a question is formulated in one of the following ways: What is the probability of at least ... What is the probability of *not* ..., you can be certain that not only the correct answer but also its complement will appear among the five answer choices. For example:

What is the probability of getting at least one head when flipping a fair coin three times?

The answer choices could look like a) $\frac{1}{8}$ b) $\frac{3}{8}$ c) $\frac{1}{2}$ d) $\frac{3}{4}$ e) $\frac{7}{8}$ You could do the calculation and we will, but you could also reason like this: Answer choices a) and e) are complementary and c) is complementary to itself. One, two, or three heads would work, so the probability should be high. e).

To solve the problem, we note that there are four possibilities: 0 heads, 1 head, 2 heads, or 3 heads. $P(0) + P(1) + P(2) + P(3) = 1 \rightarrow P(> 1) = 1 - P(0)$. So all we need to do is figure out the probability of getting no heads, meaning all tails. The counting begins.

1 HHH 2 HHT 3 HTH 4 HTT 5 THH 6 THT 7 TTH 8 TTT

The coin has two sides and there are three flips, $2^3 = 8$ possibilities and only one of them has no heads. The probability of no heads is therefore $\frac{1}{8}$ and the probability of at least one head is $1 - \frac{1}{8} = \frac{7}{8}$.

Student Notes:

Red | conv. | hybrid
40% | 30% | 20%

20% | 10%

$\frac{4}{10} \times \frac{3}{10} \times \frac{2}{10}$ $\frac{24}{1000}$ $\frac{12}{500}$

~~red~~ c

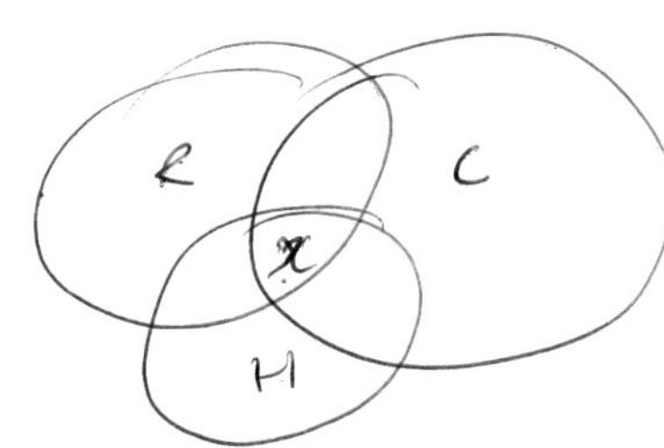

$P(R \cup H \cup C) = P(R) + P(C) + P(H) - P(R \cap C) - P(R \cap H) - P(C \cap H) + P(R \cap C \cap H)$

$48\% = P(R) + P(C) + P(H) - 20\% - 16\% - 10\% + x$ (40%, 30%, 20%)

$48\% = 90\% - 46\% + x$

$48\% = 44\% + x$

$x = 4\%$

2 cars

Chapter 12

Data Sufficiency

12.1 The Answer Choices

Data-Sufficiency questions are designed to measure your ability to:

- Analyze a quantitative problem
- Recognize relevant information
- Determine whether there is sufficient information to solve a problem

Data-Sufficiency questions are accompanied by some initial information and two statements, labeled (1) and (2). You must decide whether the statements given offer enough data to enable you to answer the question. Data Sufficiency questions do not ask for actual number solutions, and instead they ask simply: Is the information given adequate to solve a question?

Two statements are laid out as two possible conditions. It is important to analyze each statement independently from the other statement. In other words, you cannot mix the information from one statement with the other.

There are two common types of Data Sufficiency questions:

- Close-ended: Is "Y" divisible by 3?
- Open-ended: What is the value of "X"?

In a close-ended question, you can judge whether each statement is sufficient by determining if its answer is always Yes or always No. A statement is insufficient if its answer is sometimes Yes or sometimes No.

In an open-ended question, you can judge whether each statement is sufficient by determining if its answer results in a single value. A statement is insufficient if its answer leads to a range of values, instead of a specific value.

The answer choices are always the same; by the time you get to the test and have done enough practice problems, you will not even have to look at the answers if the question is of the data sufficiency variety.

Here are the five answer choices:

(1) Statement (1) alone is sufficient, but statement (2) alone is not sufficient

(2) Statement (2) alone is sufficient, but statement (1) alone is not sufficient

(3) Both statements TOGETHER are sufficient, but NEITHER statement ALONE is sufficient

(4) EACH statement ALONE is sufficient

(5) Statements (1) and (2) TOGETHER are NOT sufficient

These answer choices are mutually exclusive and complete. One of them must be true and only one can be true per question.

12.2 The Three Questions You Must Ask

Is the information in Statement 1 sufficient to answer the question *uniquely*, meaning do you know that only one answer is possible? It does not matter what the answer is: yes, no, red, blue. Will it always be the same, no matter what?

Is the information in Statement 2 sufficient to answer the question *uniquely*, meaning do you know that only one answer is possible?

If both of these questions are answered with a "No," then the third question becomes necessary: Is the information in Statements 1 and 2 together enough to answer the question *uniquely*?

When deciding whether to start with Statement 1 or Statement 2, start with the one you understand the best. That way you can get a better handle on the problem before you tackle the one you understand less well.

Remember that you do not necessarily have to solve the problem; you only need to determine whether it can be solved uniquely. For example, if you are given two linear equations:

$3x + 2y = 7, 2x - 8y = 4$. Solve for x. Two independent linear equations, two unknowns, the problem must have a unique solution for x and y. End of story. You do not care what x is. On the other hand, if the two equations were:

$2x - y = 7, -6x + 3y = -21$,

these two equations are not linearly independent. The latter equation is simply the first one multiplied by three and adds no new information. Think about it graphically: Two parallel lines will never intersect; if the lines are identical, they have infinite intersecting points. Only if the lines are not parallel will the intersection have a unique solution.

Sample Data Sufficiency Question

(Source: GMAT Mini-Test. Reprinted with prior permission.)

If a real estate agent received a commission of 6 percent of the selling price of a certain house, what was the selling price of the house?

(1) The selling price minus the real estate agent's commission was $84,600.
(2) The selling price was 250 percent of the original purchase price of $36,000.

- ○ Statement (1) ALONE is sufficient, but statement (2) alone is not sufficient.
- ○ Statement (2) ALONE is sufficient, but statement (1) alone is not sufficient.
- ○ BOTH statements TOGETHER are sufficient, but NEITHER statement ALONE is sufficient.
- ○ EACH statement ALONE is sufficient.
- ○ Statement (1) and (2) TOGETHER are NOT sufficient.

EXPLANATION:

From (1) it follows that $84,600 is 94% (100% - 6%) of the selling price, and thus the selling price, $84,600 / 0.94, can be determined. Therefore (1) alone is sufficient.

From (2) it follows that the selling price is 2.5($36,000). Thus, (2) alone is sufficient.

The best answer is the fourth choice.

12.3 Read Carefully and Assume Nothing

Whether the information is sufficient may hinge on one word in the question. It is imperative that you read carefully and *make no assumptions*. You cannot assume that a number is an integer or a positive number unless it is explicitly stated, you can prove it, or it makes sense. For example, if a problem discussed purchasing pencils, you *can* safely assume a non-negative integer number of pencils is being purchased. But suppose you were given a problem stating "Jeff and Martha are standing in line for a concert." You cannot assume that they are standing together nor can you assume that Jeff is ahead of Martha in line.

Time problems are also a potential source of confusion. For example, you may be asked to find how long a time period is and the information given is: Time period Z begins at 10 a.m. and ends at 3 p.m. You *cannot* assume that the 3 p.m. is five hours later. It could be the next day, the next week, the next millennium, assuming we still keep time that way by then. As you will discover in business school, you must read the fine print and look for loopholes. It is an eye-opening experience to realize just how much we incorrectly assume.

Another important factor is being able to discern whether you are being asked for an absolute number or a ratio. While you may not be able to determine absolute numbers for various quantities, it may be possible to find the ratio. Therefore, if you are being asked for a ratio, do not assume that because you cannot find the values themselves that you cannot find the ratio.

Practice Problems

Is there enough information to answer the question *uniquely*? Remember that you do not have to answer the question; simply determine whether you have enough information to do so.

(1) A stereo was discounted twenty percent and discounted again to reach a final sale price of \$500. What was the original price?

(2) The initial ratio of boys to girls at a concert is 1:1. After 500 more girls are allowed in with no additional boys, the ratio becomes 10:9, girls to boys. What is the total attendance at the concert?

(3) A right triangle is inscribed in a circle of radius 4. The longer side of the triangle has a length 3. What is the length of the short side?

(4) If $xy > 0$ and $y > -3$, is $x > 0$?

Student Notes:

Chapter 13

MBA Admissions in a Nutshell

13.1 Overview of MBA

A Master's in Business Administration (MBA) is an advanced degree offered by most business schools to college graduates who (preferably) have a few years of work experience. MBA coursework teaches students essential skills for the corporate world by focusing on both technical (e.g., finance and economics) and personal (e.g., leadership and management) abilities. Earning an MBA has become an essential step in establishing a successful career in the business world. Some companies are willing to sponsor their employees' education, either while they are working part-time, or during a hiatus from their employment (with a contract to return afterwards).

Today most business people in management positions have MBAs. While it is possible to achieve success in the business world without an MBA, not having a degree from a top business school can be a severe handicap because so many people continue their education and training. Both the quantitative and qualitative skills taught in MBA programs are qualities that are in high demand in the real business world. If you decide not to pursue an MBA, it is possible that you are making a decision that will hinder your future success in the corporate world.

Although the MBA is the common name for a graduate management degree, many institutions offer the same program with another name such as Master of Management (MM), Master of Public and Private Management (MPPM), Master of Administrative Science (MAS), and Master of Science in Business Administration (MSBA), to name a few.

13.1.1 Why MBA

There are a multitude of reasons why so many people now consider an MBA to be an integral step in their career paths. Just having an MBA can make the difference between a high-paying, high-power job, and an endless cycle of unsuccessful interviews. Statistics show a pronounced difference in salary between graduates of top MBA programs and the MBA-less (on average the former earn as much as twice the latter). There is also a substantial gap in pay between those with MBAs from top schools, and those who graduate from lower-ranked institutions. Because the stakes are so high, seeking expert advice and meticulously preparing your application are essential for your future success at a top business school.

Increased salary is only one of the benefits of an MBA from a top business school. Job flexibility and security, the opportunity to make important connections, enhanced upward mobility, and the satisfaction of doing more interesting, significant work are just a few of the reasons why hundreds of thousands of applicants attempt to gain admittance to business school each year.

Entrepreneurs often seek MBAs before they strike out on their own so that they can learn from business professionals who have already succeeded. This gives them a greater chance of success in the real world. An MBA provides both a qualification that will help further your career path and a body of practical knowledge. This combination of credentials and expertise will help you achieve your goals regardless of the profession you choose.

During your years in business school, you will meet many people, some of whom may prove to be valuable contacts later in your career. The establishment of a broader network of contacts is one of the reasons why it is important to go to a top business school. The better the business school, the more valuable those contacts are likely to be.

Interacting with a network of well-trained and educated business contacts while in school is also excellent practice for your re-entering the business world full-time post MBA. Working closely with others and finding common ground with your fellow students provide you with training for any future positions with much higher stakes. By then your business and interpersonal skills could mean the difference between winning and losing a multi-million dollar contract with an important client.

13.1.2 Academic Offerings

Business schools, in general, make special efforts to simulate the actual business world in the classroom by:

- Creating lessons from actual situations
- Using the very computer programs you will need to use in the business world
- Involving you and your fellow students in active discussion of problems so that you will better understand how to interact with people and be more skilled at working in a team to develop the best solutions.

Academic expertise varies from program to program. There are some basic topics in the areas of management and business which all schools will cover. But if your area of interest is less common, you will need to inquire about the course offerings at each specific school. For example, some schools have a focus on Operational Management while other schools are known for their MBA training for non-profit organizations.

In addition to detailed curricula which you can either find on-line or directly request from schools, there are three major teaching methods used by business schools: lecturing, the case method and the project method.

Once you begin your initial research on business schools, you will often hear the term "case method." The case method, developed by the Harvard Business School faculty in the 1920s, refers to creating a more authentic business environment in the classroom through the study of actual cases in which business decisions were required.

The case method involves classroom discussion of situations in which students are required to face and react wisely to the challenges of the business environment. This is now the preferred method of teaching at many business schools around the world. However, depending on the subjects and the level of courses, some schools offer more of a lecturing method than the case method.

This is certainly something to consider when making your business school decisions. By using the case method, the professors facilitate discussion, give their observations, and lead the class but do not focus on lecturing. A significant portion of classroom time will be taken up by students, and their answers to the professor's questions and analysis. If you are not comfortable in an interactive classroom environment and are not interested in becoming more comfortable in such an environment, it may be wise to consider schools that do not use the case method so much. However, if you are interested in a classroom setting in which you actively discuss cases and develop and analyze possible solutions verbally, then consider schools that emphasize this teaching style. This information should be readily available either in brochures or on school websites or from conversations with students, faculty, alumni or admissions officers.

Developed on a similar premise to the case-method form of study, the project course involves the creation of solutions in addition to decision-making and discussion on the part of students. These courses are generally devoted solely to the analysis and research of one project and the solving of that project for a hypothetical business entity. Needless to say, such courses require a great deal of time and hard work.

You may have heard a lot of discussion regarding student project teams. Depending upon the school you attend, you will spend lots of time working with other students to develop solutions to class assignments. Teamwork allows students to better understand themselves and how to interact with colleagues. It often leads to the development of well thought out and interesting solutions to problems.

In addition to curricula and teaching methods, you will want to assess what the faculty will offer you. In general, the quality of the faculty can be determined by the reputation of the school itself. Yet, you may also want to consider the amount of time faculty spends on teaching vs. pure research, the priority the school assigns to teaching vs. research, and the major research areas in which faculty members are specialized. In order to make an accurate assessment, you must explore and evaluate the classroom experience of students.

You may find a wide spectrum of elective courses within each business school that go beyond the typical business school fundamentals. You may also want to consider some joint overseas study or internship programs through your business school. In your investigatory research, you will find that each program has its special features that distinguish it from others.

Another possibility you might want to consider during your MBA is simply taking courses outside of the Business School at which you are studying. The opportunity that you are granted during the MBA program is in part simply the opportunity to return to an academic environment and explore. Do consider, even if you are not going to commit yourself to a dual-degree program, expanding your horizons by taking or sitting on courses outside of the typical Business School curriculum. However, you should not engage in outside courses if they significantly digress from your current studies.

13.1.3 Pre-MBA Checklist

If you are considering a more intensive, for example, one-year or 18-month program, it is likely that you will be expected to come in with a solid background in certain relevant subjects, such as Economics and Math. Many schools provide summer boot camps prior to the start of official coursework to refresh the memories of students in those areas. The traditional two-year MBA programs also expect you to be comfortable with Calculus and Economics and even certain elements of Accounting prior to the start of their programs. For this reason it is important that you are aware of prerequisites for courses and possibly take some courses on your own before your MBA.

You will be expected to have solid computer skills when you arrive at a school and to further develop and enhance them during your tenure in your program. If you are not completely comfortable with computers and computer programs, it will be helpful to you to have some crash course on Microsoft Office applications before entering school.

Communication and people skills are two most important skills required of a good manager. Refreshing your fundamental grasp of English to make yourself articulate, well-spoken, and well-versed in business expressions will make you fit in faster and better in a variety of settings including group meetings, conference calls, and presentations.

Manhattan Review is keenly aware of these pre-MBA training needs and therefore has developed a series of intensive courses to help the entering MBA students become well prepared for all the challenges ahead during their MBA study and job search. Please email us at info@manhattanreview.com or call us at (212) 997- 1660.

13.2 Program Types

13.2.1 Traditional Model

MBA Programs are designed in several different ways. Each program has its own unique rules and philosophy.

The traditional MBA model requires its students to take certain core requirements in their first year and to take elective courses in their second year. This model enables student to establish a solid background in the fundamental areas of the study of business and explore particular areas of interest in their second year of study

Generally, schools identify themselves with certain areas of expertise. In order for you to specialize in a particular area, you typically will need 5 courses within a specialty. For individuals with strong math and accounting backgrounds, it is possible for them to be exempted from certain courses and thus be able to finish their degree more quickly, but such exemptions occur strictly on a school to school basis. Such an exemption allows you either to finish early or to take more advanced level courses. Again, this will depend upon the specific guidelines of a particular program.

13.2.2 Accelerated Programs

One year programs, despite the name, typically last a year to a year and a half. In general, all students in your program are on the same track. They have the advantage of making smaller investment of time and money than two-year programs. However, they often lack the opportunity to specialize. Many European business schools offer one-year programs. In the US, some top business schools also offer accelerated MBA programs in addition to the traditional two-year track. For example, Johnson Business School of Cornell University offers a one-year MBA program for students with other advanced degrees. Columbia Business School offers a one-and-half year MBA program for students with significant work experience or other advanced degrees.

13.2.3 Part-Time MBA

Besides traditional full-time MBA programs, some schools also offer part-time, dual degree and distance learning programs for you to earn your MBA in the most optimal way based on your interests, lifestyle, and individual preferences.

Some students choose to do their MBA part-time while working full-time. We recommend that you take time to thoroughly consider the pros and cons of this approach.

Part-time status has the following main advantages:

- You can lessen the financial burden of getting an MBA by working your way through school.

Part-timers have the opportunity to gain marketable skills from business schools without the large financial sacrifice full-timers make. Part-time study accompanied by full time work may be an option, if the financial commitment required by Business School is larger than what you are prepared to make. Some employers assist employees who are willing to work and study in funding their tuitions.

- You can advance along the same career path on which you started.

Individuals who don't wish to change careers may find the part-time MBA an excellent option. But if you are entering Business School with the intention of changing careers or even if you are just open to changing careers, keep in mind that it is difficult for part-time students who have been consistently working in one field to change fields. Part-time students rarely have the opportunity to do summer internships and thus prove themselves in a new area. They also frequently are not given as much attention by the career services centers of business schools, as they are, at least, working. In addition, when companies conduct on-campus recruiting, frequently part-time students as a result of their working schedule are unable to attend.

Before settling on part-time study, you will also want to consider the long and hard hours of homework and classroom time and the difficulties that can arise when you combine work and study. Be certain that your company is supportive of the endeavor. For example, when you have a paper due or a final exam, will you be able to devote time to studying and writing or will you be given, regardless of your involvement at school, a consistently large load of assignments? In addition, you will need to consider the stress of your current position as well as the time commitment.

Remember: There are only so many hours in a day. In addition, a part-time MBA can take as many as four years to complete.

Please be aware that part-time students tend not to get the same treatment as full-time students. Sometimes full-time students are privileged in terms of spots in courses and, simply as a result of having more time and a flexible schedule, they are able to get to know professors better. In a similar sense, part-time business school students have fewer opportunities to network and their jobs tend to prevent them from enjoying all that a program has to offer—i.e. opportunities to actively participate in clubs, opportunities to attend events (recruiting events, parties, lectures).

As a means of making the part-time MBA status work well for you, we suggest

- Excellent time management
- Do not drag out the process, take enough classes (though not excessive) to enable you to finish in a timely manner
- Make friends, especially attempt to connect with some fellow part-time students
- Remember that if part-time is too frustrating, you can switch to full-time status
- Make time for yourself to relax. Three to four years without weekends is too much to take.
- Try working from home occasionally.

Pros	Cons
• Save Money	• Fewer Career Options
• Keep Job	• More Limited Network
• Do Not Have To Move Your Family	• Smaller Increase in Salary
• Earn MBA	• Lots of Work; Maybe Very Stressful

If being a part-time makes sense financially and professionally, you should do it. You will in the end have the same degree as your fellow full-time students. You will also have accomplished the not-so-easy task of balancing work and study, a marketable skill. You will have had the opportunity to get to know your fellow part-time students and through them to develop some valuable connections.

Another option is to begin as a part-time student and end as a full-time student. That way you can make yourself more available at the end when it seems to be the most intensive period for seeking post-business school positions.

13.2.4 Dual Degree MBA

Joint-degree programs offer you the opportunity to get through two degrees at once, much faster than you would finish them separately. More than that, dual-degrees offer you the unique opportunity to diversify your background through the study of two disciplines in which you have an interest and witness where and how these disciplines overlap. A JD/MBA program is a very common dual-degree. But there are many others.

There is a variety of dual-degree programs from which you may choose. Some students view the dual-degree program as an opportunity to gain expertise in range of disciplines. From school to school, the programs vary. You can combine a Public Health master's degree, a Medical degree, a Law degree, or an International Affairs degree with an MBA. Certain schools have established excellent dual-degree programs.

One thing that dual degrees do offer is the opportunity to specialize—an opportunity so rarely available in a typical MBA program. Dual degree programs provide you with the ability to have more of a focus on something. This is particularly useful for candidates who know precisely what they want to do.

The dual-degree in another sense offers greater flexibility. You may find yourself uncomfortable in the business world but, with your JD/MBA, you have the luxury of being able to fit in faster with more ease. Though a dual degree is more expensive than a straight MBA, it is less expensive than attaining the two degrees separately.

Keep in mind also that there are not many slots allotted for dual degreed individuals. In addition, be aware that depending on the particular fit and position a company is looking for, hiring managers sometimes do not consider a dual degreed individual to be a more qualified candidate than the straight MBA graduate. Instead they consider dual degree as more of an alternative path and therefore less of an appropriate fit for their opening.

Take a moment and consider what you will do with a dual-degree before jumping into one. This will be both a financial commitment and a commitment of additional time in school. You will need to consider where you want the degree to take you and if the combination will suit those needs. Will this combination provide you with additional opportunities or limit them? Will the degree increase your earning potential or limit it?

For some students, the financial commitment in itself may be enough to deter them from engaging in a dual degree program. But for others, they may find that the dual degree offers them a diverse experience, a chance to be a part of two worlds and an ability to gain knowledge in a field that will work as a complement to their business and management skills. On average, less than 10 percent of MBA students seek an additional degree. However, the dual degree may be just the thing you want.

13.2.5 Distance Learning

Many schools offer distance-learning programs. In these programs you attend courses, often online, or through occasional trips to campus throughout the year. The duration of MBA programs can vary greatly but generally they are self-paced.

While distance learning programs lack direct exposure to and interactions with faculty and students, they can have the benefit of allowing you to be flexible about where you live and work as you pursue your MBA.

Distance learning MBA programs also grant you the same degree as your full-time MBA or part-time MBA colleagues earn and often at a lower cost.

13.3 MBA Programs

13.3.1 US MBA Programs

Traditional Business School programs in the United States are two years (actually 21 months) long. From the Ivy-League to lesser known regional business schools, high quality business education is available to individuals with a range of different backgrounds. MBA programs in the US generally require an undergraduate degree and some work experience.

The following is a list of some the most well-known US business schools:

Columbia Business School
Cornell S.C. Johnson Graduate School of Management
Dartmouth College – Tuck School of Business
Duke University – Fuqua School of Business
Harvard Business School
M. I. T. Sloan School of Management

Northwestern University – Kellogg School of Management
NYU Leonard N. Stern School of Business
Stanford University – Stanford Graduate School of Business
UCLA Anderson School of Management
University of California, Berkeley – Hass School of Business
University of Chicago
University of Michigan – Stephen M. Ross School of Business
University of Pennsylvania- The Wharton School
University of Virginia- Darden School of Business
Yale University – Yale School of Management

Compared to these top MBA programs with nationwide brand name recognition, regional schools are the kind of institutions that enjoy a significantly higher profile and recognition in their local region than across the country. If you are interested in working in a particular area, it may be wiser seeking out a school that is highly regarded locally than going for a top-ranked Ivy League MBA program. This may allow you to both save money on the education itself and be able to establish the right connections to achieve your professional goals. In some regions the alumni networks of certain local institutions may prove to be highly supportive and effective in a job search process.

13.3.2 International MBA Programs

If you are interested in working internationally, you may want to consider the possibility of earning your MBA degree outside the United States. It will open your horizons to new places, new cultures and new professional and personal networks. You may have the opportunity to learn another language. Attending business school abroad in itself will make your MBA a unique experience. It will potentially enable you to get positions which require a degree of international expertise more easily than your counterparts from US business schools could. You will not only have lived abroad but also studied business abroad.

You may also have the opportunity through US schools such as Wharton, Chicago and Columbia to do a portion of your MBA abroad. This may also help you gain some degree of real life international exposure in addition to developing international connections while studying for an MBA in the US.

There is a wide range of different kinds of institutions overseas. Each institution carries its own unique philosophy and organization. A wide range of companies recruit at European and Canadian business schools. Again each school is different and you are going to want to check the specific school you are interested in to get information on who recruits at that school.

The following is a list of some well-known European and Canadian business schools:

Bocconi University School of Management – SDA Bocconi
Copenhagen Business School
Cranfield School of Management
ESADE Business School
HEC - Montreal
HEC – Paris
Henley School of Management
IESE University of Navarra
IMD – International Institute of Management and Development
INSEAD
Instituto de Empresa
London Business School
Oxford Brookes University
University of Cambridge Judge Institute of Management
University of Lancaster – Lancaster Business School

University of Manchester – Manchester Business School
Oxford University Said Business School
University of Strathclyde Graduate School of Business UK
Warwick School of Business
Western Ontario

13.3.3 MBA Rankings

Rankings provide a simple way of determining the quality of education of a variety of programs. The most prominent Business School rankings are the following:

- *Business Week*
- *Financial Times*
- *US News and World Report*

However, applying to schools simply based upon rank is not the best way to judge the excellence of MBA programs or whether a particular program is appropriate for you. Rankings do not tell the whole story. We recommend that you look beyond rankings to make your decisions about business schools.

• Rankings benedit nationally known schools.

U.S. News and World Report and *Business Week* do not rank regional programs. If you are interested in working in your region, it may be just as beneficial to seek out a school that is highly regarded in your local area. This may allow you to both save money on your education itself and be able to make the connections necessary to achieve your professional goals. In some regions, the alumni networks generated by certain local institutions may carry greater weight than a degree from a nationally ranked school.

• Ranking statistics are not as precise as one might like to believe.

If graduates of one school are making average starting salaries of $100,000 in London, and graduates of another school are making average starting salaries of $70,000 in St. Louis, what does 100,000 tell you as an average? As costs of living vary so much from location to location, a dollar amount indicating average salaries is somewhat misleading.

• Most rankings present some degree of bias.

They rely on the opinions of individuals. The biases of corporate recruiters or of alumni themselves will no doubt be reflected in rankings.

With regard to rankings, please keep in mind:

- Many items are left out of the analysis.
- A lot is not accounted for and disregarded.
- AND things change.

13.4 Application Strategy

The value of an MBA from a top school is indisputable. Therefore, you should give yourself the best chance for success by putting as much effort as possible into your applications. But first, you need to evaluate your personal strengths and weaknesses to determine which schools fit you best.

13.4.1 Where to Apply

From the US to Asia to Europe and other locations, you have a number of business school options. We recommend that you consider where you want to be before beginning the actual application. Schools have their own particular atmospheres, climates, geographies, cultures, in addition to having unique curricula, expertise, and rankings. Before simply applying to the highest-ranking schools according to *U. S. News and World Report* or *Business Week* or the *Financial Times*, take a moment to consider the following questions.

Where would you like to spend a few years? Often the pursuit of prestige and the attempt to be accepted at the highest ranked school possible (though important in some respects) get in the way of selecting a school that is right for you. What areas would you like to specialize in? How do you learn best? Do you prefer teamwork to working alone or vice versa? Are there individuals at a particular school with whom you are interested in interacting? What are your chances of getting in?

You should weigh carefully what a school offers both academically and environmentally. This may require some degree of thought and research. Ultimately, the decision will involve analyzing the uniqueness of the programs that you are interested in applying to and thinking about who you are and how MBA programs are related to your professional and personal inclinations. A good method of analysis is simply prioritizing the most important features you are looking for in an MBA program and then creating charts and/or lists with columns dedicated to those criteria.

For example, Joanne is interested in the following criteria: (1) class size, (2) rank, (3) curriculum, (4) length of study, (5) location (East coast), and (6) expertise in finance. In order to measure her options in an organized fashion, she selects several business schools and inputs their characteristics on a chart. You may want to try filling in Joanne's chart as a practice assignment.

School	*Class Size*	*Rank*	*Curriculum*	*Length of Study*	*Location*	*Expertise in Finance*
Yale						
Wharton						
Stanford						
INSEAD						
Columbia						
NYU						
UT Austin						
UC Berkeley						

We do not recommend applying to too many programs. The crafting of too many applications can act as a hindrance to your own ability to create customized applications for each program. In addition, every application incurs a financial cost. However, how many is too many will vary from applicant to applicant.

The students with whom you will be studying are often just as important to your overall MBA experience as the faculty. Most schools post on their websites and in their informational brochures statistical information on their entering class, outlining where students are from, what professions they have been involved in, their age range and years of professional experience. From these statistics, you can gain a basic understanding of how well you will fit in to the school's environment. Think about yourself in relation to these class profiles. Do you see yourself thriving amongst these individuals? Do you fit in? In addition, you may want to keep in mind the class size. Do you enjoy the energy of lots of people or prefer intimacy of a smaller learning group? We recommend that you visit the school and observe the atmosphere in order to better understand whether or not you will be comfortable there.

As a means of scaling down your list of programs, we recommend the following tactics:

• Try to eliminate those programs that are poorly suited to your strengths and weaknesses.

If a program is geared toward international business and you have every intention of returning to your hometown to run your father's restaurant, then that program can be omitted, as you may not gain what you are looking for from that program.

• Gauge your likelihood of acceptance.

No precise formula exists to determine if you will be admitted. Talking with admissions officers, individual students enrolled in a program, or your own friends and colleagues will aid you in measuring your likelihood of acceptance. Manhattan Review's Admissions Consulting staff is at your service to assist you in this matter.

• Do not be afraid to apply to a few schools that you doubt you will get into.

Your doubt could merely be a symptom of your own lack of confidence.

13.4.2 When to Apply

As a rule, apply as early as possible. At most schools this will increase your chances of admittance. Many schools have very few spots available for the third round of admissions.

Some schools make public the numbers of applicants they accept per round. You may want to examine such statistics to help you determine when the best time to complete your applications is.

If you have already submitted applications to MBA programs and were not accepted at the schools you wanted to attend, you should consider applying again. In fact, second-time applicants tend to have a better chance of admittance to B-School than first time applicants do. But in order to reapply successfully, you will have to reconsider how you want to present yourself to the admissions committee.

The best way to increase your chances of success is to improve your application. This could mean diversifying your work experience or preparing for and retaking the GMAT, a very important factor in MBA admissions, or it could mean choosing different individuals to write recommendations for you. If you applied late the first time, reapplying early significantly increases your likelihood of admittance.

In this matter, every individual is different. You must take some time and consider your whole application and what you could do to improve it. Most likely you will notice strengths and weaknesses. You will need to think about how the weaknesses could be improved. If, for example, your GMAT score is in the low range for the school, preparing for and retaking the GMAT is a good idea. You may want to ask someone you trust to evaluate your application and point to problem areas. Manhattan Review's GMAT Preparation courses provide you with the skills and strategy you need to do your best on the exam.

Reapplying is easier than applying for the first time. Often schools allow you to carry over references and reapply with just one new reference letter. However, you may consider more than one depending on what you think will best help you in this process.

In your essays you will want to point to how you are a better candidate now. What have you learned in the time since you last applied? How have you grown? In what ways have you changed so that the school will value you more?

Manhattan Review's Admission Consulting team is made up exclusively of graduates from top Ivy League schools. Our team is ready to carefully guide you through the admissions process.

13.4.3 Program Materials

When you request information, we advise you to request not only a brochure but also a course catalog if possible. This will enable you to gain a deeper sense of the school's academic offerings and what it focuses on. Then you can compare that to other schools you are interested in attending. Some of this information may be accessible online. Some schools offer CD-ROMs with such information. In general, we recommend that you get as much information as possible so that you will be able to make as informed a decision as possible with regard to where you apply.

Visiting the school is perhaps one of the best ways to make your decision. When visiting, we recommend that you take the opportunity to speak to current students, tour around the campus and make detailed observations. Could you imagine yourself studying there?

Part-time students may have the opportunity to take a course before enrollment. This may be a good idea especially if you are uncertain of whether you want jump into an MBA at this point in life.

13.4.4 Talking to the Right People

It may also be helpful to speak with corporate recruiters regarding the strengths of an individual program and the degree to which they favor candidates from certain programs over others. After all these are the individuals who will be making the ultimate hiring decisions. It is also useful to understand why these recruiters value individuals from certain schools. It may be because of the expertise of the schools or simply their reputation.

One of the best means to determine the quality of a program is to measure the success of its graduates and assess their reputation in the corporate world. If you have the opportunity to do so, the best way to find them out is to consult with business people, inquire about which graduates they find impressive and which they do not. This will offer you insights into the long-term and short-term successes of graduates. Keep in mind that success varies from individual to individual, but business schools should ideally grant their students the means to progress, change, grow, adapt, and move towards career goals. The more solid a program is in terms of content and reputation, the more successful its graduates are.

The following questions may prove useful in more casual or exploratory conversations with students, alumni, faculty and recruiters as well as in your interview.

- What kind of impact has your MBA had on your career?
- In what ways does the material you studied in school assist you in your position?
- Are you confident about hiring people who attended your program?
- Were your professors approachable and open to student contact?
- In terms of administrative support did you find the school supportive? Did you and your classmates find positions easily?
- What were the other students in your program like?
- What were those most challenging experiences during your MBA years?

One of the most attractive reasons to do an MBA is the quick improvement in salary and in career opportunity. It is for these reasons that you must find out which companies recruit at which business schools. Statistics on post-graduate salaries do not tell the whole story. You must inquire into where MBA graduates are working immediately after graduation and how their careers progress years down the line.

You should also inquire about the following areas:

- Internship Opportunities and Job Placements
- Recruiting Companies & Industries
- Salary Potential and Ranges
- Reputation in the Business World
- Variety of Career Options – Sectors and Mobility
- Long-term Career Path
- Short-term Career Opportunity

In your consultations with admissions committee members, students, faculty, and alumni, you should also try to determine how helpful the alumni network is and the types of opportunities offered by alumni.

13.4.5 MBA Books and Forums

There are a number of books out there that offer suggestions as to how to engage in the process of applying for an MBA. Most of these books only brush the surface of MBA experience and potential MBA programs. However, these books may offer some assistance in familiarizing yourself with the process and the reputation of certain schools.

One good way to learn about MBA programs is through large MBA forums organized by various organizations. For example, TopMBA offers World MBA Tours all around the globe. Going to a forum is an excellent way to improve your knowledge of MBA admissions procedures, to encounter representatives from schools, to meet other interested students, to simply gather brochures and application materials for programs that interest you, and to directly ask school admissions staff specific questions.

In addition, schools host their own information sessions in various international cities where you can speak directly with school representatives, attend seminars, get an interview, and familiarize yourself with the school's philosophy and interests.

13.4.6 Funding Options

One of the most difficult aspects of the MBA decision is money. How in the world can you afford it? We in general advise you to apply for any scholarships you happen to be qualified for and then devise a plan for funding your MBA once you know how much money you have available to you and where you have been accepted. An MBA in the US can cost up to $60,000 a year. But you have options. To support yourself and cover some of your own expenses, you should consider part-time work. Summer internships between your first and second years are often very well-compensated in terms of helping you save up for your cost. There is a tremendous number of scholarship opportunities overlooked every year as well.

Most MBA students take out loans. Counting on the greatly increased earning potential after completion of the MBA, students tend to find loans the simplest funding option. Federal loans are the best type of loan you can get. You may take out no more than $18,500 from the Federal government per school year and the rest will need to come from private institutions, such as Citibank, Access group and the GMAC.

The financial aid offices of the schools you are applying to are in general quite helpful in assisting students in locating the best option. Scholarships, grants, and part-time work are all options to help finance your MBA.

13.4.7 Women Applying for MBA

The ratio of men to women in MBA programs across the nation is far from equal. Not many women elect to apply for MBAs despite the opportunities an MBA provides, i.e. high salaries, effective connections and career advancement. Why not? Why go to other professional schools and not Business School? Some women have hesitated to pursue MBAs as a result of the competitive nature of the programs, despite the fact Law School and Medical School are perhaps more competitive. Ultimately, it seems that it is the time and the commitment required of traditional post-MBA consulting or investment banking careers that most family-minded women find hard to accommodate.

Despite various hesitations and doubts women may have about pursuing an MBA, they rarely find their experience to be an inadequate one. In general, the overwhelming majority of women find themselves satisfied with their business school experience and their new opportunities. More and more women are pursuing MBAs.

13.5 MBA Applications

Business school applications generally contain 8 basic elements:

(1) GMAT Scores

(2) TOEFL scores (for non-native English speakers)

(3) Essays

(4) Recommendation Letters (2-3)

(5) Undergraduate/Graduate Transcript(s)

(6) Interview

(7) Resume

(8) Application Form

These application elements are not listed in any particular order, as some schools pay far more attention to a particular aspect (e.g., the GMAT score) of your application and other schools give greater weight to another portion of the application (e.g., the essay portion). However, all items are an integral part of the package you present to the school of your choice, and therefore, all items must be taken seriously. The entire application should aid the admissions officer in developing a clear vision of you, identifying your strengths and weaknesses, where you have been and are going, and the difficulties you have overcome.

The length of the MBA application process varies for every individual. It is preferable to begin this process early. This enables you to have enough time to make each element of your application the very best it can be. The range of time spent on the entire application process spans anywhere from 6 months to 2 years. Preparation usually means first taking the GMAT and TOEFL (for non-native English speakers), gathering applications, beginning the process of thinking about why you want to engage in this commitment and what you will have to offer to business schools, deciding where to apply, updating up your resume, writing essays, and preparing for interviews.

We recommend the following basic method of completing the application process:

(1) Prepare for the GMAT / TOEFL (for non-native English speakers) exam(s)

(2) Take the GMAT / TOEFL (for non-native English speakers) exam(s)

(3) Gather applications

(4) Determine which schools to apply to. Research, visit, talk to students, alumni, admissions etc.

(5) Update and polish your resume

(6) Solicit recommendations

(7) Write essays

(8) Complete other application items—personal information, resume, short answer questions etc.

(9) Proofread and edit application with a high degree of attention to detail

(10) Send in applications on time

The final decision regarding your application will be made based not on one element alone but upon the application as a whole. For example, perfect essays alone will not get you in. There is no precise formula for predicting whether or not you will get into to a particular program. A lower range GMAT score does not equal rejection nor do a few bad grades in undergraduate courses.

Many factors play into admissions decisions such as essays, recommendations, GMAT scores, transcripts, work experience and personal experience. So try not to sell yourself short. In addition, there are some helpful rules to go by in the MBA admissions process. The admissions officers are looking for individuals who have attained excellence in the workplace, in academia, and in their private lives. You have the opportunity to demonstrate your full capacity through the elements highly valued by admissions officers.

We recommend you apply to no more than 6 schools per round of admission and those schools should be a good blend based on your various priorities and likelihood of acceptance. This will allow you to give your best to those applications and customize them to the programs to which you are applying. Being able to dedicate your time to the specifics will make the difference between acceptance and rejection.

Our Admissions Consulting staff members are all recent graduates of top Ivy League schools and committed to getting you into the schools of your choice.

13.5.1 Application Form

Each school requires an application form. The form requests general personal information (e.g., your address, phone number, name, short answers to background questions). We recommend that you familiarize yourself with the application form early in the admission process. Most forms can easily be filled out online or in print.

Within the application, other application information (recommendations, essays, resume, etc.) is also required. Please be advised that early awareness of any unique information required by the school will allow you to avoid last minute panic.

You should begin your application by first deciding on a systematic approach. Manhattan Review's admissions consulting staff can help you to develop the appropriate method for customizing your application.

13.5.2 Transcripts and Test Scores

All schools require copies of your transcripts.

We recommend requesting undergraduate as well as graduate transcript(s) early in your application process. Some institutions take up to 8 weeks to process requests for transcripts.

Be aware of the precise way the schools you are applying to want to receive transcripts. Do the schools want the registrar to sign across the seal of the envelope? Do the schools want the transcript mailed directly from the undergraduate/graduate institution? If there are any particular requests, do let your undergraduate/graduate institutions know about them in advance.

Besides the GMAT scores which are required of all applicants (please refer to our GMAT in a Nutshell for more information), non-native English speakers also need to take The Test of English as a Foreign Language (TOEFL) to attend undergraduate and graduate institutions at which English is the primary language of instruction, if they don't have a diploma from these types of institutions already.

The TOEFL is a Computer Adaptive Test (CAT) designed to test your grammar knowledge and English vocabulary. It may be taken at a date of your convenience at an official testing center.

The original version of the exam includes 4 sections: listening, grammar, reading, and writing sections. After September 27, 2005, the US TOEFL exam will undergo some changes including, most notably, a new oral section. The new test is designed to allow universities and colleges to better evaluate how well students will perform in an actual classroom.

In Europe and Asia, the exam will remain in its old form until 2006. In the winter of 2006, the new form of the exam will gradually begin to be disseminated to testing centers throughout the world.

Although the TOEFL exam is largely a test of language ability, there are certain test-taking strategies that will ensure that you do your best on the exam. Through expanding your vocabulary and concentrating on areas of grammar and usage that are particularly difficult for you, you can improve your English and your TOEFL score.

Remember that the actual exam is on the computer. So make best use of chances to take Computer Adapted Tests (CATs). For many test-takers, reading large amounts of material on the screen not only dries out their eyes but makes it hard to absorb the material. Simply practice reading on the computer. The only way to improve is to practice and learn from your prior mistakes.

13.5.3 Resume

Not every school requires a resume. However, most schools offer the option of including a resume with your application. A resume may help you further match yourself with the school.

- **A resume should use strong verbs.**
  Use words like 'founded, started, created, developed, managed.' You also want to be sure to diversify your use of verbs throughout your resume.
- **Make sure that your resume highlights the strongest elements of your work experience, educational experience and activities.**
  If, for example, you attended prestigious institutions and/or worked for prestigious companies, make sure the admissions officers notice this. Or, if the positions you held at particular firms were noteworthy, this should stand out on your resume.
- **Your resume should ideally be 1-page.**
  Do not repeat yourself. Each word should add to the overall impression you are seeking to give the admissions committee.
- **A resume should look appealing to the reader.**
  The formatting and font should be easy on the eye and help give the reader an idea of who you are.
- **The resume should be a flawless, error-free document.**
  Your resume must demonstrate a consistency or dedication so that reviewers can follow your progress or transition in a profession or some special interest. For example, it may be a consistent involvement with France, a consistent position in finance, or consistent extracurricular pursuits.

Of equal importance is the breadth of your experiences and interests. Use your resume to demonstrate your interest in and commitment to a variety of disciplines or areas, as diversity and expanded horizon are highly valued by business schools. The goal is to show an admissions committee precisely what you have accomplished in your academic, professional, or personal lives.

You may also consider including slightly more information than you normally would in your resume. If your former employer is not well recognized nationwide or by admissions officers, we suggest that you offer some brief description of company background and its major milestones. For example, you should emphasize its most important business aspects such as its revenue size, personnel size, products, services, international locations, rankings, among others.

In addition to describing the company, describe your role within the company. Include your individual responsibilities and accomplishments. The more specific description, the greater the likelihood it will differentiate you from other applicants.

In general, your resume provides another way to further develop and emphasize those qualities and subject matters you are seeking to highlight in your application. If time allows, spend some time working on tailoring the resume to fit each institution. Emphasize the aspects of yourself that the school seeks. Certain schools will indicate precise items they want in the resume. Be sure to be attentive to those items and include all information they request. Again the resume should stress the overall skills and traits that all business schools look for:

- Ability to prioritize and manage time
- Academic achievement
- Adaptability
- Critical thinking skills
- Dedication
- Eagerness to participate
- Enthusiasm for Business / Management Study
- Goal-Oriented
- International/Global exposure
- Management Experience / Leadership / Entrepreneurship
- Optimism
- Originality / Creativity
- Qualitative and Quantitative Skills
- Sincerity/Integrity

13.5.4 Recommendations

Recommendations are often a source of stress for even the most qualified of applicants. It is an important part of your application, that is, to some degree, out of your hands. But do keep in mind this is a variable all applicants must encounter, not just yourself.

It is important that you develop relationships with your superiors both in the professional and academic realms so that you have some individuals upon which you can rely for recommendations. As a general rule, it is best to select people who know you well and like you and then do your best to make it easy for them to get the recommendation done as soon as possible. If you can, sit down and talk with them about your plans and send them all the necessary material.

Be sure they have your resume indicating your past activities so that they are aware of your past achievements and your future goals and plans. You might even want to send them an essay from your application stating your purpose in applying.

You may want to select individuals who know a variety of positive aspects of your personality. For example, you might select someone who has witnessed your management abilities in the business world, another individual who has seen your intellectual capacity and communication and writing skills in an English course, and another who knows of your quantitative abilities from an

Engineering course. Or you may select those individuals who know a particular aspect of your character. Like your essays, your recommendations should also be matched to the schools.

Make sure your recommenders are aware of your deadlines. Contact them every so often to make sure they have all the necessary information.

13.5.5 Essays

Essays are important. It is in your essays that you are able to explain yourself. All the time you spent thinking about why you want to attend Business School and why you feel ready to do so now will pay off in the essays.

We **recommend** the following method of tackling your essay:

- Match yourself to the school.
- Determine what the question is asking.
- Consider how to answer the question: Brainstorm.
- Organize. Select the aspects of yourself to emphasize and back them up with examples / stories / anecdotes from your experience. Put this information into an outline format which you find comfortable.
- Write the essay, paying attention to format.
- Make revisions.
- Have someone read it over.

Manhattan Review's admissions consulting team can offer you expert advice on essays and the application process.

The guidelines around which we suggest engaging in the essay writing process are the following:

- Convince your reader
- Distinguish yourself
- Demonstrate sincerity
- Write in a fashion that keeps the reader's attention

To do this we suggest the following:

(1) Select different and unique, but honest experiences. You may want to expand upon an experience to make it seem more unique. Try to select those experiences that make you a unique candidate.

(2) Convey your experience honestly. The admissions committee will notice the difference between extreme embellishment and sincerity and depth.

(3) It is in your writing that you have the opportunity to demonstrate your personality. One important way of doing this is through your style. Within your essays you want to continue to keep the reader's attention. Try to use the 1st person singular, use "I" and avoid "we". Avoid using the passive voice as well as the 'to be' verbs.

13.5.6 Interview

Nowadays interviews are, if not required, highly encouraged. It is not necessary to be interviewed on campus. In general, interviews are easily arranged in most major cities in the US and abroad. In general, interviews are scheduled to be 30 minutes long but many applicants find the meeting going longer especially at schools to which they are accepted. Performing well at an interviewing is a skill; it must be practiced. By focusing on some of the likely questions you may be asked, reviewing your applications, so as not to contradict yourself, and thinking over again how your experience has led you to want to go business school, you will be able to come across as an intelligent, committed, knowledgeable individual, ready to be a part of the schools for which you interview.

An interview is a test of those skills not so readily apparent in the other parts of your application—are you a good communicator, are you charming and able to relay your passion to others verbally? Schools seek applicants who are strong on paper as well as in person. Following the interview, the interviewer generally sends his or her recommendation and/or evaluation to the school.

Schools are interested in discovering your degree of interest in them and whether you are truly a candidate who has something to offer the school at this point in your career.

Here is a summary of **the most important things** you have to know about interviewing with a business school.

- **As you have already done for your application, make sure you have done your research.**
  Your interviewer will quickly be able to distinguish between an applicant that has developed some understanding of a school's background and one that has not.
- **Practice interviewing for Business School with a friend or colleague.**
  Talk to people on the admissions staff to learn more about the school. This will also help you become more comfortable discussing the school and yourself.
- **Think of good questions to ask your interviewer.**
  This is a good opportunity for you learn as well! Think of interesting questions and match them to your interviewer.
- **Write a Thank-you note.**
  Be sure to mail a thank-you note either on the day of the interview or the day after your interview.

Important things to Avoid:

- **DO NOT BE DISHONEST.**
  People can read through such dishonesty quickly.
- **DO NOT BE UNPREPARED.**
  Do your research. Talk to people. Practice interviewing.
- **DO NOT DEMONSTRATE INCONSISTENCY.**
  Both in your answers at the interview and in your application, do not give the interviewer and thus the school any reasons to think you are flaky and fickle.

13.6 Application Techniques

As important as where you apply and when you apply is how you apply.

13.6.1 Stay Organized

First, be as organized as possible. By being organized we mean creating a systematic approach to putting together your application. Do not leave anything out. In the absence of just one element of your application, your application will go unread. By implementing an organized approach to the process, you can bypass last minute panic.

By missing an application item, you significantly hurt your chances of admittance into a program. For that reason, please be as organized an applicant as possible from the beginning: make lists, track steps and create an approach that works well for you.

Below is an example of a table that you may consider using as an organizational guide. You can make it a checklist or include in it more detailed information such as the particular essay questions or the names of the individuals who are writing your recommendations for those particular schools etc.

School	*First Date of Preparation*	*Deadline*	*Transcripts*	*GMAT*	*Essays*	*Recommendations*	*Resume*
Yale							
Wharton							
Stanford							
INSEAD							
Columbia							
NYU							
UT Austin							
UC Berkeley							

13.6.2 Explore Ideal Candidacy

You should emphasize the right aspects of your personality. As each school is looking for different strengths in their applicants, you need to look into what the school focuses on or is best at or is famous for in order to determine what aspects of yourself to underscore. However, there are certain qualities which all business schools find important.

- Ability to prioritize and manage time
- Academic achievement
- Adaptability
- Critical thinking skills
- Dedication
- Eagerness to participate
- Enthusiasm for Business / Management Study
- Goal-Oriented

- International / Global exposure
- Management Experience / Leadership / Entrepreneurship
- Optimism
- Originality / Creativity
- Qualitative and Quantitative Skills
- Sincerity
- Strong communication skills

You should present these positive personal traits of yours clearly and powerfully in your applications by tailoring the content for each school. For example, you lived in Lebanon and Kenya as a child and have been working in Tokyo for the past 4 years after receiving an undergraduate degree in the US. Now you are applying to a school that highly values international exposure. Even if you listed those international experiences in your resume or other parts of your application, you probably would be making a huge mistake by not underscoring the exposure, the learning and new values you have gained from those unique journeys.

Most business schools tend to look for a class that represents a variety of professional and personal backgrounds, but some schools favor applicants who come from specific areas of expertise. For example, financial backgrounds may be favored by Wharton whereas international experience is favored by Columbia.

The following table provides a sample list of most sought-after qualities of MBA applicants from hypothetical business school programs.

MBA Programs	*Quality #1*	*Quality #2*	*Quality #3*
Elite Business Schools	Dedication	Creativity	International Experience
West Coast B-Schools	Quantitative Skills	Enterpreneurship	Communication Skills
Euro B-Schools	Leadership	Management Skills	Academic Achievement

You must do a good amount of work to determine how to rank these qualities. You will in effect create a ranking system yourself. Rankings, such as those done by *Business Week, U.S. News and World Report* and the *Financial Times*, may provide a useful starting point.

In order to better understand the preferences of particular business schools, it is helpful to spend ample time researching their websites, looking at the student profiles of their incoming classes, visiting the schools and discussing with admissions staff or current students the things they feel the school values most. Evaluate the direction the school is taking you through its application requirements as a whole, in particular, with its essay questions.

Please do your homework thoroughly on each school and be mindful of the particular traits and professions valued by the school. This is an important process. If you fail to precisely gauge what a school most values, it is unlikely that your application will match with what that school is looking for. Meantime, uniqueness is always appreciated. Please always highlight the specific aspects of your uniqueness in all your applications.

In addition, Manhattan Review's Admissions Consulting staff is made up exclusively of graduates of top Ivy League business schools and they are committed to your success. Their expert advice will help you discover which schools are right for you and enable you to get in to those programs.

13.6.3 Tailor Your Approach

You will need to define a method to match your qualities, values and desires to those of the schools. The process of defining this method and writing essays that highlight these elements will be beneficial to you for the business school application process as well as for your own personal and professional growth.

You will need to think further to define those parameters precisely. For example, dedication has different meanings for different schools to which you are applying. You also need to explore how important each school thinks dedication is in relation to the many qualities an applicant might possess. Dedication can have a variety of meanings: perseverance, commitment to certain values and principles in life such as work ethics, commitment to carrying through a task with high quality, commitment to detail, among others. But it is your task to find the meaning that is right for the schools to which have chosen to apply.

After engaging in the process of research and discussion with alumni, students, faculty and admissions staff, we discovered that it is dedication that the Elite School of Business and Management most values. Here for illustrative purposes, we will start the process of tailoring an application around the emphasis of dedication.

For the Elite School of Business and Management, to be dedicated, one must:

- Commit to a short-term or long-term goal or task
- Continue to do it for a long time
- AND ideally achieve or exceed the objective.

We also list out our definitions for other qualities highly valued by Elite.

Qualities	*Definitions*
Dedication	Commitment to a goal; Stay persevere by continuing working towards the goal for an extended period; Demonstrated ability to achieve the goal.
Creativity	The ability to think out of the box and come up with new and executable ideas.
International Experience	Extensive travel or work experiences aboard with an open mind to different cultures.

After coming to an understanding of which qualities a school values, in what particular order they value them, and how that particular school interprets the meaning of those qualities, you can begin to match their ideal profile to your personality, interests and experience.

13.6.4 Evaluate Your Experience

Now you must perform a thorough self-evaluation and think deeply on your past. What are those experiences you should highlight in your application? Brainstorming may help you recollect personal experiences that might be highly valued by the school. The goal is to generate a detailed list of your relevant experiences.

In the initial brainstorming stage, neither limit nor judge yourself. Simply jog your memory for unique challenging experiences and you may be surprised by what you remember. Experience means both personal and professional experience. It is often the more personal aspect of experiences that a school will find unique. Do not limit yourself to the business world. Take some time to think about particular elements of those experiences. It will be useful to detail each element in writing. If this selection process proves difficult, ask for help. Consider talking to parents, friends, siblings, mentors, relatives, as they may remember elements of your past that you have forgotten. In addition, Manhattan Review's admissions consulting staff is made up exclusively of graduates from the top Ivy League business schools and committed to your success. Their expert advice will help you recall and select the experiences that will be most favorable to your application.

For example, Joanne made a summary of relevant experiences as a result of her brainstorming exercise. The following table provides an example of both experience and hobbies associated with dedication in the order of priority.

Relevant Experiences	***Rank Based on Relevancy to Dedication***
Accounting Firm (from junior auditor to manager)	1
Volunteer work (a summer teaching the disadvantaged children)	2
President of Rugby team (after reorganization)	3
Tennis coaching (at club)	4
Study of Philosophy	5
Worked while in college on construction site	6
Competed in Marathon	7
Volunteered at Food Kitchen	8
Volunteered at Hospital	9
Volunteered at environmental cleanups	10

In general, you are going to want to select the experience that is the most closely matched to the qualities that the program to which you are applying seeks. It must in and of itself speak to the reader, without an in-depth description of why this experience demonstrates this quality. However, you must elaborate on the uniqueness of that experience in your writing.

13.6.5 Prove Yourself through Essays

You will need to consider who you really are. You should present yourself in a truthful manner. Any dishonesty or stretching of the truth will not lead to a coherent application. Thus, you must determine what your true strengths are and match those traits with the schools to which you are applying. If your strengths really do not resemble the ideal student profile of a school, we suggest that you seriously consider applying elsewhere.

You must understand what each question is truly asking. One major mistake applicants often make is not answering the question. This should be avoided at all cost. If the question asks: "How did your past experiences lead you to want to attend Harvard Business School?" Do not simply list your past experiences. You must explain them and how they caused you to make Harvard Business School a committed choice of yours.

This may appear rather simple but some schools write questions that require a greater attentiveness to the way the question is phrased than others. Other questions require leaps of imagination to demonstrate creativity. In such situations, it is wise to be creative and to say something that other applicants would not, again within the bounds of your own particular background. This will make you a more unique applicant.

Design a way to answer the question. If, for example, you are answering the question asked on Stanford's application for its 2005/2006 entering class: "What matters to you most and why?" You are going to reflect on your true passion. Is it running your own firm, helping people, achieving your goal, making a difference, or others? You should also be able to substantiate your choice of passion with concrete and consistent examples of your past efforts.

Once you have selected aspects of your character to emphasize and established solid examples to back them up, it is recommended that you compile this information into an outline before writing. The outline will help to guide your writing.

Now you are ready to write. The writing itself needs to be readable and clear. Be conscious of what you are trying to express. If you get lost, refer back to your outline.

In your essay, you should emphasize the setting of the place where your experience took place, the challenges you were facing over a period of time, and your plan and actions to overcome the hurdles. You must also indicate what you gained from it. Do your best to explain at greater length how you personally dealt with the hardships of the position. This explanation in itself will lead the admissions committee to an appreciation of what you learned.

As a result of your work and devotion, you will need to show what came of it. Over your time with the accounting firm, did you receive compliments from clients? Were you staffed on assignments of higher profile or with greater challenges?

By thoroughly accounting for what you have done and achieved and showing difficulties you have overcome, you will develop fitting, interesting, and well-supported answers to questions. Everyone has his or her own uniqueness. You must discover it, explore it, and develop it in your essay.

Keep in my mind that you have a limited amount of space to explain yourself. Be efficient with that space. Repetition should be kept to a minimum. But every aspect of yourself you are seeking to highlight should be explained in full. Don't be afraid to delete portions of your essay that prove to be redundant.

When you begin writing, format your essay in a clear manner. For some applicants this means bullet points, for others lists, for others creating subheadings. You must allocate an exclusive period of time to concentrate on the writing. There are many things to remain aware of when moving from a rough draft to a final version.

- Use several different types of sentence structures/words. Again do not repeat yourself too much.
- Be sure you are using strong verbs (not too many 'to be' verbs)
- Pay attention to the style, the voice. Read the essay aloud to yourself to make sure it sounds good.
- Do not neglect format
- Correct all spelling errors
- If you have not already done so, tailor the essay to the school. Mention the schools' particular curriculum, professors, location and your relationship to it.
- Be sure there are no inconsistencies among different essays and between the essays and the rest of your application
- Correct any punctuation/grammar mistakes
- In addition, though application essays often contain personal information, it is advised that you let at least one friend read it over for content, clarity and grammar.

13.6.6 Ace Your Interview

After you have submitted your application, the Admissions Committee writes you a letter inviting you to an interview with one of their highly regarded alumni. The Admissions Committee gives you the names of 3-5 individuals to call. You decide whom you would like to call based purely on their names and the year of graduation. Or perhaps you will have to call several in order to come up with a meeting time that works for both of you.

We recommend that you schedule your interview as soon as possible in order to avoid later conflicts.

Here is an example of an interview notification letter.

> Dana Miller
> 2020 Sunset Blvd.
> Los Angeles, CA 90210
>
> Dear Dana,
>
> After receiving your application, we have decided that we would like you to meet with one of our highly successful alumni. Please contact:
>
> Heather, class of 1990, 700-700-7000
> Shannon, class of 1995, 800-800-8000
> David, class of 2004, 900-900-9000
>
> We ask that you schedule the interview as soon as possible so that we can give you our decision as early as possible.
>
> When you have contacted one of the individuals listed above, please let us know online or via email the name of the person with whom you are meeting and the time and date of your meeting.
>
> We will make our decision after receiving feedback from your interviewer and reviewing your application again. In general, our decision will come approximately 8 weeks after we have received your application. Please call if you experience difficulties in scheduling with these alumni.
>
> Regards,
>
> James Jaffy
> Interview Coordinator

Your interviewer may ask you for a copy of your resume at the interview and may not. Your interviewer, provided the interview is during the week, will be dressed in professional clothes. You should wear appropriate interview attire regardless of the time of day or the day of the week.

You should be prepared to answer at an interview. As in the other sections of your applications, establish the qualities you want to emphasize before the interview. This will add to the coherence and consistency of your interview and entire application. Your answers should be thoughtful, reflective and consistent. They should demonstrate the personal traits in you that are highly valued by admissions officers. Prove yourself to be an easy person to talk to and be able to explain your background and your interest in business school with ease.

General Background Questions:

- Tell me about yourself.
- What are your short-term and long-term goals?
- What sets you apart from the rest applicants?

- Why B-School? Why now? What do you think you will gain from it?
- Why are you interested in applying to our school?
- What are those major criteria when you selected the schools?
- Why did you choose your undergraduate major?
- How will an MBA from our school help you specifically?
- Where else are you applying?
- Why those schools?
- Why did you decide to apply to x number of schools?
- What school is your first choice and why?
- If you are not accepted anywhere you applied this year, what will you do?
- Do you have any specific questions or concerns about our school?
- What are your strengths and weaknesses?
- How will you improve your weaknesses?
- Who do you admire and why?
- What books are you reading?
- What is your favorite book or film and why?
- What do you do with your free time?
- What do you enjoy doing most? Why?
- What leadership roles have you taken on outside the business world?
- What have you accomplished in these roles?
- What obstacles have you encountered?

Questions Related to Prior Work Experience:

- Have you spent much time abroad? Tell me about an important experience you had away from home.
- What did it teach you?
- In your personal life, name a moral dilemma you encountered and explain how you resolved it.
- What is your current occupation?
- What do you do there?
- What are your responsibilities?
- What is difficult about your position?
- Describe a typical day.
- What are the driving factors of your choice of your current job and your planned career path as a whole?

- Why did you pursue this position?
- Do you like it?
- What do you dislike about it?
- What have you accomplished in your current role?
- What have you failed at?
- What could you do better?
- What leadership roles have you been in at your current position?
- What have you done or suggested that resulted in a change in your company / department / group?
- How do you rank among your peers?
- How do you relate with your superiors?
- Where do you see your company and industry moving in the future?

Questions Related to Prior Educational Experience:

- What undergraduate institution did you attend and why?
- How did you do?
- What did you study?
- What were you best at?
- What if anything would you change about your undergraduate experience?
- What did you most appreciate about your undergraduate experience?
- What clubs, sports or activities were you involved in as an undergraduate?
- What accomplishments did you have as an undergraduate?
- Did you work to support yourself as an undergraduate?

It is also likely your interviewer will ask you some out-of-the-ordinary questions. There is no way to be prepared for every question. For this reason, you should be yourself and simply ready to think. Ask the people with whom you practice interviewing to ask you some strange stuff. This will help prepare your mind to answer tougher questions. Here are some examples:

- Why should we take you?
- How would those who work under you describe you?
- What do you think about the war in Iraq?
- What do you think about Mayor Bloomberg?
- Tell me how you would like to help the world. What charities do you see yourself donating to as a successful businessperson?

Again, despite your lack of preparedness for certain questions, you will want to speak honestly and confidently, prove yourself to be a person who is informed about the Business School and able to answer questions spontaneously and thoughtfully.

Interviewers prefer questions in which you demonstrate knowledge of the particular MBA program as well as an interest in the interviewer. That means, be sure, in as natural a way as possible to ask questions about the interviewers experience at that business school or an informed question about the program. Here are some examples, though we strongly encourage you to come up with your own original questions:

- How do I best prepare for the program at your school?
- What did you like most about your time at the school?
- What were those best courses you attended at the school?
- How involved the faculty members are in teaching?
- What was your class like? Was there a strong sense of community?

Here is an example of an interview.

HEATHER (INTERVIEWER): Tell me about yourself—professionally and personally.

DANA (APPLICANT): I am from Los Angeles. I was born and raised here, went to XYZ college after graduating from ABC high school, and have worked for three years after college. I spend lots of time doing volunteer work in my old neighborhood. Initially, I worked on a local program to help kids make it through high school and then I took over managing that program and then I started a similar volunteer program at School #51 nearby. But I have done a good deal of traveling. As a college junior, I studied abroad in China, and during high school, spent a semester in France ...

HEATHER: I see you attended the University of Southern California, and there, you studied Economics. Why did you choose USC and why did Economics appeal to you at age 18?

DANA: Yes, I went to USC because my father went there and I have always had a deep respect for him. Also I am committed to this community and wanted to stay nearby.

And Economics, well, it was new to me and I enjoyed the course. One particular professor really made those graphs come alive for me and I was good at it. I did take a variety of other courses in the sciences mostly.

HEATHER: What are the strengths and weaknesses of USC and the Economics Department? If you had to study again, what courses would you take that you did not take? Languages? Sciences? What clubs would you participate in that you did not?

DANA: The economics department was strong in econometrics, but weak in developmental economics... I began volunteering in college and eventually became president of the volunteer association. I am a bilingual in Spanish and English. But I studied lots of Science—Biology, Chemistry and Physics in school. If I had to study at the college again, I would take more Humanities courses, more Philosophy and Literature, as I have recently come to understand the value of such disciplines in understanding human nature.

HEATHER: Why do you want an MBA from AAA Business School? Why now?

DANA: I have chosen AAA Business School because of its strong expertise in the area of General Management, Corporate Ethics, its location, and its reputation of academic excellence.

HEATHER: What other schools have you applied to? Why these?

DANA: I have applied to BBB Business School because of their reputation for strong international studies. I am interested in working in this community, but that does not preclude seeking knowledge of other places and expanding my horizons. I think it's wise to learn about others as well as ourselves. However, AAA remains my first choice as I feel there is a stronger fit between the program and myself.

HEATHER: Describe any management positions you have been in and how you met the difficulties.

DANA: During the time I managed the volunteer organization located in West Hollywood, I encountered a lot of different kinds of people. Different ages, nationalities, and class and racial backgrounds. Each person required a slightly different approach. Through patience and perseverance, I have learned how to improve my interpersonal skills, how to make them feel comfortable, how to understand their concerns and goals, and how to encourage them to work with you.

HEATHER: If you came to AAA Business School, what activities do you see yourself being apart of?

DANA: I see myself start up a volunteer club at the school perhaps teaching or tutoring in the public schools. I am also interested in becoming apart of the Society Club and hosting gatherings and fundraisers.

HEATHER: And where do you see yourself in 20 years?

DANA: I see myself playing a significant role in a local responsible company with strong values of corporate responsibility and fairness.

HEATHER: Anything else you would like to tell me about yourself.

DANA: I am not purely optimistic and idealistic. I realize the problems existent in the corporate structures today and realize that on these will be very difficult to change...

HEATHER: Well, Dana, what questions do you have for me?

DANA: Why did you choose AAA? ... How has your MBA helped you in your career path?

After your interview, your interviewer is supposed to contact the admissions committee and submit feedback very shortly after the interview. For this reason, please be advised that you should send your thank you notes the day of the interview or at the latest the day after the interview.

Your interviewer will offer commentary on your ability to communicate thoughtfully and clearly and present yourself well. They may comment on your English skills, if you are a non-native English speaker. This does not mean you should worry about every grammar mistake you make. But simply take time to speak as freely and as well as you can. They may comment on whether or not you come across uncertain, confident or arrogant about your self-assessment and future plans. Other areas the interviewer needs to assess include your knowledge of the program, your competitiveness as a prospective job applicant, your team-working skills, and the value you will bring to the class as a student and to the school as an alumna/e. At the end, the interviewer needs to rank you on a scale against the applicant pool and write a recommendation to the committee including any specific reservations, if there are any.

Here is a hypothetical case. Suppose Dana did an excellent job in his interview with Heather. Within 2 days of the interview, Heather submitted her assessment report to the admissions committee:

Dana was articulate, enthusiastic, confident, convincing, well-prepared, and realistic. He has demonstrated his managerial abilities through the successes he has had in his professional positions and his organization of volunteer programs. I was especially impressed by his enthusiasm coupled with his insights of the issues currently facing corporations and governments today. I believe he would make an excellent MBA student at AAA and recommend him wholeheartedly. One of his goals is to work in the area of Corporate Social Responsibility. Though, often times, a more extensive liberal arts background or knowledge may be required in that area, I think that he demonstrated a sincere interest in and a strong dedication to creating a more responsible corporate culture through his own volunteer work. He also applied to a few other institutions in the same league as AAA. He indicated that AAA is his first choice due to its location near his family and friends, its focus on Corporate Ethics and its diverse student body. I think he would make a valuable contribution to his class. Professionally, I felt that due to his young age, he may need more working experience, but with that experience I see him growing into an excellent colleague. I highly recommend Dana to the Admissions Committee of AAA Business School.

To summarize, here are some **golden rules about interviews**.

- **Practice a few basic questions in advance.**
- **Speak clearly and intelligently.**
- **Dress appropriately.**
- **Be polite, courteous, and natural.**
- **Send a thank-you note.**

Student Notes:

- Cancel South Africa
- Study for GMAT – in Dec
- Apply for HBS now
  - INSEAD
  - &
  - Columbia

After

- DCF – growth of the cash flows
  – base case scenario
- Comps – ?
- Others – many business / goldmine!
- Exit analysis –